The Best Medicine

T0235731

Bruce L. Gewertz • Dave C. Logan

The Best Medicine

A Physician's Guide to Effective Leadership

 Springer

Bruce L. Gewertz
Department of Surgery
Cedars-Sinai Health System
Los Angeles
California
USA

Dave C. Logan
Marshall School of Business
University of Southern
California
Los Angeles
California
USA

ISBN 978-1-4939-2219-2   ISBN 978-1-4939-2220-8 (eBook)
DOI 10.1007/978-1-4939-2220-8

Library of Congress Control Number: 2014954633

Springer New York Heidelberg Dordrecht London

Printed on acid-free paper

Springer is part of Springer Science+Business Media (www.springer.com)

This book is dedicated to our wives, Diane and Harte, who provide the leadership in our lives.

Acknowledgments

In researching this book, we carried out structured interviews with more than 50 leaders from all sectors of healthcare across the United States. Their willingness to candidly share their experiences and insights were selfless and invaluable. Some are quoted by name in the text; in other situations, the sensitivity of the scenarios required anonymity. Regardless, their enthusiasm and contributions are the essence of whatever value the work has and we are deeply grateful.

We have both enjoyed superb personal mentoring through our careers. Each of us has a key mentor who shaped our views; sadly both are deceased. Warren Bennis provided wise and always stimulating counsel to Dave. At every juncture, he was supportive, constructive, and personally committed. Bruce had the great opportunity to work and bond with David B. Skinner while at the University of Chicago and afterward. David was a superb role model who generously advanced his colleagues' interests ahead of his own. Both men received much recognition during their lives; their influence will continue not just in our work but in that of the many others they shaped and inspired.

To be complete, a number of other friends and colleagues provided wise counsel on these topics through the years and reviewed the text in preparation. At the risk of missing a few, we would like to specifically mention Steven Lorch, David Skaggs, Harry Sax, Bryan Croft, Michael Ruchim, Steve Sample, Patti Riley, Beverly Kaye, Bill Cohen, John King, Steve Zaffron, and Tom Cummings.

From the Editors

Physician leadership is changing quickly. To keep our comments relevant, we have an addendum on our website (www.therightmedicinebook.com) that focuses on the specific needs of physician leadership in private practice. Our web site has additional resources, including ways of contacting both authors.

Contents

Chapter 1
Leadership as Personal Capital

Perhaps, you are reading this book because you are beginning a new administrative or leadership post, or you are merely contemplating one. While we believe the material will benefit you in those pursuits, we also believe that the insights and behaviors that contribute to successful executive leadership are, in fact, the same as those that ensure a productive work life and personal life in general. Your leadership capabilities could be viewed as personal capital, the increase of which can enrich all pursuits.

Regardless of our professional duties, in order to be effective and resilient in our personal life, we will time and again be required to demonstrate leadership. In times of trouble, we must rely on our ability to properly adjust our performance to provide a clear direction for friends or family. As succinctly stated by U.S. Naval Commander Michael Abrashoff as the title of his book: *It's Your Ship*. Leadership skills allow you to sail that ship.

Leadership is an intrinsic human asset, not a by-product of a title or administrative appointment. We will show you through real-life examples that one's innate leadership abilities can be improved with thoughtful changes in attitudes and behaviors.

B. L. Gewertz, D. C. Logan, *The Best Medicine*,
DOI 10.1007/978-1-4939-2220-8_1,
© Springer Science+Business Media New York 2015

The Leadership Challenge

For the past 25 years, we have had the privilege of serving in a number of leadership positions in academic and healthcare organizations, as well as consulting with numerous companies. While the dynamics of these professional organizations (law firms, medical groups, academic faculty, etc.) have their own peculiarities, we have seen that the motivations of these highly educated people are not that different. The majority seek to maximize two interconnected goals—**satisfaction in their daily activities** and **a sense of purpose in their long-term objectives**. In nearly every survey, regardless of the field of endeavor, these desires consistently outweigh the lure of higher compensation and even that of personal recognition.

If one accepts the validity of these observations, the job of an enlightened leader in professional organizations is simple—create a workplace in which the largest number of well-intentioned and skilled professionals are allowed to exercise their skills and are convinced that their efforts contribute to a worthwhile end. In word and deed, *aspirational leaders* reinforce that belief. While they acknowledge the rational self-interests of their colleagues, such as career advancement and higher pay, they focus far more of their efforts on making consistent strategic decisions rather than fine-tuning organizational charts or compensation plans. Openness is a key element. They are comfortable sharing their thoughts, not just within an insular executive group, but across the organization as a whole.

When leaders succeed in these two most important tasks (which we could summarize as *value-driven decision making* and *transparency*), their colleagues can pass the "wake up in the middle of the night test." In other words, even if summoned from a deep sleep, all members of the organization can speak to what the group is trying to accomplish and how they plan to get it done. This book is intended to provide both a theoretical framework for such leadership and specific management techniques to achieve it.

Given the proliferation of academic work on the subject, there is no shortage of ideas as to what the essential components of leadership are. Our leadership model focuses on characteristics that can be applied consistently, whatever the setting, and that are capable of inspiring the kind of unconventional thinking that will be required in this period of "creative destruction" in medicine.

Key Attributes of Leaders

Based on our extensive interactions with a wide range of leaders in health care and medicine, three personal attributes are demonstrated time and again. Successful leaders are nearly always genuine and optimistic in their attitudes and resolute in pursuing personal fulfillment in work and life.

Being Genuine

We can all enumerate virtues that make our relationships with others go more smoothly. Most of us would include kindness, empathy, engagement, and honesty in the list. We can also probably agree that even with the best of intentions, we occasionally fall short in living up to these ideals of behavior. Nonetheless, if our behaviors *on the whole* are consistent with those higher values, our friends, family members, or colleagues generally accept infrequent lapses without much consequence. In short, they know us well enough to not change their opinion based on an isolated incident.

In a work environment, it is not always possible to rely on a long history with someone to smooth out interpersonal conflicts. Especially in leadership positions, we interact with a large number of people who we may know only slightly or not at all. It is, therefore, essential that leaders project positive behaviors that are both convincing and real to strangers and friends alike.

There is only one way to do this consistently—by displaying external behaviors that are fully concordant with one's internal feelings and attitudes. We call this being *genuine* or *authentic* in our interactions with others. While some may represent themselves well for relatively short periods of time without a deep connection to their intrinsic motivation, invariably the truth is revealed and reputations and effectiveness suffer mightily. Leaders we spoke to repeatedly pointed out that most people have a well-developed sense of when someone's words and behaviors are insincere and do not reflect what they are thinking and feeling. One senior leader remarked that, for him, remaining authentic is a primary focus of all his public and private interactions. He specifically asks his confidants to speak up if ever they feel his external message has strayed from his core values.

Despite the importance of being genuine, we are not advocating some standard methodology for communicating successfully. Your method for connecting with others must be consistent with your intrinsic personality and style. Part of personal growth is learning to put ourselves in situations where our specific mode of communicating is most effective. Steve Jobs found his niche in carefully staged large-group presentations anchored by his enthusiasm for the technology he championed. Jack Welch was most effective in small-group sessions in which his down-to-earth message of individual accountability could be delivered directly.

Being genuine is most important when things do not go so well. A number of clinicians working in oncology and high-risk procedural specialties noted how much more effective their interactions became with families suffering loss when they were open to sharing their own disappointment in the outcome without being defensive. Similarly, when business reversals occur, leaders need to communicate their messages without pretense or excuse.

The Power of Optimism, Tempered by Realism

The importance of an optimistic attitude in work and life is hardly a new revelation (see "The Power of Positive Thinking," Norman Vincent Peale, 1952.). However, the effects of an optimistic attitude on all aspects of human endeavor and on health are now even more clear, thanks to several remarkable observations. A famous study by Giltay and colleagues (2004) of 941 men and women aged

65–85 years used a detailed questionnaire to separate the subjects into groups based on their disposition—optimistic vs. pessimistic. The influence of optimism on life-span was nothing short of remarkable. A total of 70% of the most optimistic men lived 9 years past the beginning of the study, while only 40% of the least optimistic survived the same interval. This effect was seen in women as well (although slightly attenuated) and held true even when cardiovascular risk factors and other health measures were accounted for.

Further support for this effect is provided by data from the so-called Nun Study, most recently analyzed by Dunner and colleagues. Investigators had access to the handwritten autobiographies of 180 nuns, which were prepared when they entered their convents beginning in 1930. Entries were blindly coded for emotional content (i.e. positive, neutral, or negative in tone). All-cause mortality was tracked late in their lives. The investigators found that a positive attitude, expressed early in life, was a clear marker for greater longevity.

In a dissenting view, Frieder Lang and colleagues (2013) followed 40,000 adults through a decade and noted those with a darker outlook lived long. The reason appears to be that more pessimistic individuals, especially older and infirmed, sought to deal with the realities of their situation rather than cover them over with false optimism.

This seeming paradox has been explored by Tim Vogus and colleagues (including Karl Weick) with the phrase "emotional ambivalence." In high reliability organizations, they suggest, the mindset most descriptive of positive outcomes is one that anticipates a positive future, while also searching for problems before they occur. Drawing on the classic Victor Frankl book *Man's Search for Meaning*, the literature in behavioral economics and his own work with Steve Zaffron in *The Three Laws of Performance*, Dave has suggested an alternative phrase: "optimistic terror."

The best organizations and careers arise from balancing the tensions between the positive effects of optimism and the vigilance born out of pessimism. Of particular concerns is the hectic pace of life in general. In most surveys of full-time workers in the western world, those in the United Kingdom and United States work the longest hours by far. In 2003, one study by the Organisation for

Economic Co-Operation and Development documented that U.S. and U.K. workers exceeded the hours worked by those in Europe by 25% with mean hours of 2,000 per year in the U.S and U.K. (approximately 40 h per week) in comparison with 1,700 per year in Europe (approximately 30 h per week). We can agree that most physicians would exceed those numbers substantially. Surveys performed by the Pew Foundation over many years show conclusively that a hectic pace, associated with long hours and overlapping activities, clearly and adversely impacts personal satisfaction. In their most recent survey, only 27% of people who felt they were always rushed in daily life described themselves as "very happy" as compared with 42% of those who said they almost never felt rushed.

Finding Fulfillment at Work and Play—the Phenomenon of "Flow"

The feeling of rushing around, which could be defined as urgency without importance, is the single defining characteristic of many of our lives. Whether we are frantically checking our smartphones or mesmerized by yet another cable news program, we too often spend our time on details and urgencies that lack much meaning. To avoid this treadmill, prominent psychologist and a former University of Chicago colleague, Mihaly Csikszentmihalyi described a more purposeful ideal for our life, which he calls "flow."

Flow is characterized by complete immersion in a complex activity that is intrinsically motivated by our own talents and interests. The initial observations of this phenomenon were made in surgeons, athletes, and musicians who train for years to reach the high level of skill necessary for superior performance. In detailed interviews, all described a similar sense of clarity, serenity, and even ecstasy when purposefully engaged in the most challenging and difficult activities. While flow shares some surface characteristics with urgent tasks, it is elevated by the matching of hard-won skills and innate talents with a meaningful and noble purpose. Csikszentmihalyi argues that true happiness is found in those who can find a way to maximize the time they are in "flow" in their personal and professional lives.

Of most interest to physicians, Csikszentmihalyi noted that in order to remain in "flow" the challenge of tasks and the skills to achieve them both need to increase over time. Thus, what brings "flow" early in one's career may not be sufficient to maintain it.

Approaching this from a slightly different angle, Herzberg, Easterlin, and other social psychologists have wrestled with the factors that contribute to happiness in work environments. They divided the elements of personal satisfaction into **extrinsic rewards**—such as salary and administrative titles—and **intrinsic rewards**—such as improvements in the nature of work, achievement, recognition, and personal growth. In a large number of situations, it appears that the relationship between income and happiness (extrinsic rewards) follows a characteristic pattern that has become known as "the hedonic treadmill." In this construct, increases in compensation from a low starting point initially have a highly positive relationship to personal satisfaction, but once a relatively high level of compensation is reached, further increases in salary have little effect.

The pattern seen for increasing intrinsic rewards is different. Workers in a wide range of professional and nonprofessional jobs report progressive increases in satisfaction, as the nature of the work becomes more rewarding on an experiential basis. As later outlined by Warr and others, these improvements in the job environment can include opportunities for greater personal control of working conditions, the chance to use a wide range of skills in a variety of tasks, supportive interpersonal relationships, and the articulation of clear requirements, coupled with the ability to meet them.

What We Know About How Professionals View Their Jobs

It is fair to ask—does this academic research play out in real life? One of the best examples was reported by Marshall Goldsmith, who interviewed more than 200 high-performing executives from 120 diverse companies as part of a research project on employee retention sponsored by Accenture. The critical question was, "If you stay with this company for the next five years, why will you stay?" The answers were simple:

"I enjoy this work."

"I like the people I work with."

"The organization is giving me a chance to do what I really like to do."

When Bruce served as Chair of the Department of Surgery at the University of Chicago, he had the great good fortune to work closely with Harry Davis, who is a senior professor in the Graduate School of Business. Among other things, Harry is interested in the motivations and attitudes of different professional groups and spent considerable time assisting the department. In preparing for one of the yearly retreats, Bruce asked him to meet with a wide range of faculty members to get an independent sense of their enthusiasms and concerns. He scheduled 30-min interviews with approximately 20 faculty members at all academic levels. As might be predicted, not a single interview was finished in the time allotted. Promised relative anonymity, they were happy to talk about their likes and dislikes of their jobs and the environment.

In putting it all together, Harry Davis was struck by the strong positives and negatives, which were, at times, expressed simultaneously. In one sense, the glass was half full; faculty members were committed to their academic missions, relished their personal autonomy, and found great personal satisfaction in their teaching and clinical activities. Still, the same people also described areas of significant dissatisfaction (the half-empty glass). They bemoaned what they saw as a "culture of expendability" in which their contributions might be valued during their tenure but would be inevitably forgotten with their replacement. They also described a mentality that Professor Davis termed "shattered dreams." They felt they had studied long and hard in college and medical school and worked tirelessly during residency and the early part of their practice only to be faced with diminished authority within the healthcare system. In short, no amount of extrinsic rewards such as pay or recognition could adequately balance this decreased personal control of their time and activities.

For several years, Bruce kept an index card with Professor Davis' findings on his desk and referred to it whenever dealing with dissatisfied colleagues. He was impressed with how often their specific complaints and day-to-day frustrations were, in fact, triggered by the more universal concerns they described and how frequently the path to resolving their issues began with acknowledging and helping them address these larger issues.

We have found one overriding truth in our management experience with a wide range of professionals. It is simple. **The more we allow them to perform their most valued services unimpeded, the happier they will be.** These effects on personal satisfaction are far more powerful and long-lasting than would be if we merely increased their take-home pay. As succinctly stated by Brown and Gunderman, who carefully examined physician satisfaction: "to increase fulfillment of physicians, we need to ensure that the intrinsically fulfilling aspects of work are accentuated not suppressed." This can only be done by enabling all types of professionals to exert responsible local leadership and linking them to a strong network of motivated colleagues.

The successful physician leader must sustain this atmosphere despite the perplexing and, on occasion, turbulent environment of today's healthcare. The magnitude of the task makes the leadership challenge ever more important and also requires that the characteristics of effective leaders are manifest at multiple levels of the organization.

It is our hypothesis that physician leaders mature through five distinct stages of development. Each stage has specific skills to be gained and pitfalls to be avoided. Understanding these forces more completely should contribute to mastery. Let's see, if we can convince you.

Chapter 2
Phases of Physician Leadership

Physicians have the raw materials for great leadership: high intelligence, drive, and a generalized idealism toward the profession of medicine. The challenge for physicians who aspire to outstanding leadership is to continue to "own" what makes them star performers as individuals, while shifting their focus to others.

There are a myriad pathways physicians take, as they develop themselves as leaders, including pure research, clinical research and teaching, private practice, and every combination of these. Without removing any of the individual complexity of physician leaders' development, we can also see that there is an unarticulated curriculum of ascendency.

Our Approach

Our goal is to provide a useful model for physicians now and throughout their careers. Our challenge is to bring all the theory and practice of leadership together in a way that would provide clear advice for physician leaders, without "dumbing down" the subject, and to balance empirical evidence with usefulness. To

B. L. Gewertz, D. C. Logan, *The Best Medicine,*
DOI 10.1007/978-1-4939-2220-8_2,
© Springer Science+Business Media New York 2015

arrive at the advice in this book, we had to contend with two important problems.

First, the field of leadership is still young and scholars are still revising its basic assumptions. To show how far the field has come in a short period, consider this definition of leadership from a 1927 conference (reported by Moore): "the ability to impress the will of the leader on those led and induce obedience, respect, loyalty, and cooperation." Today, even basic questions of what leadership is are hotly debated. As Warren Bennis noted in 2002: "It is almost a cliché of the leadership literature that a single definition of leadership is lacking."

Second, the field of leadership is highly fractured into schools of thought, with varying levels of empirical support, theoretical grounding, and relevance to real-world problems. The result of this problem is a growing divide between the state of theory and research and the way leadership is often taught in organizational settings. It may surprise casual readers of the subject to learn that most scholars did not consider "servant leadership" to have enough empirical support to warrant large mention in literature reviews. As one telling example, Peter Northouse, whose *Leadership: Theory and Practice* is a commonly used textbook in university courses on the subject, did not include a chapter on servant leadership until the sixth edition of his book, published in 2013.

To accomplish our goal, we took an unusual approach: presenting leadership for physicians in a vertical, rather than horizontal, manner. Horizontal, as we are using the term, is to approach the subject as an ever-expanding literature review, spanning decades and inquiry methods.

Dave was the original curriculum chair for the Master of Medical Management degree at the University of Southern California, and later launched the program as associate dean in the Marshall School of Business. In his faculty and administrative roles, he began to see that the "literature review" approach to leadership was ineffective for physicians.

A different approach is to consider leadership development in a vertical context, in which people move through levels, stages, or phases. This approach informed Dave's (and John King and Halee-Fischer Wright's) *Tribal Leadership* book, which advances the view that "tribes" (naturally occurring groups of 20–150 people) advance through stages. Each stage is its own "world" of language usage, social dynamics, and political structures. A leader's job is, thus, to assess the tribe he or she is in in terms of its stage of development and nudge it along. Later stage tribes are generally more effective because they include the insights and capacities of earlier stages, while going beyond their constraints.

The vertical approach in *Tribal Leadership* is by no means new. Drawing on decades of work in multiple fields, many researchers have advanced similar developmental models. Some have proven effective and reliable (e.g., Larry Greiner's approach to organizational systems and structure) and others do not hold up to careful scrutiny (e.g., Maslow's hierarchy of needs).

Presenting a phase development model for leadership is not new. Many scholars consider Ken Blanchard's Situational Leadership to be a stage model. Jim Collins presents a stage development model in *Good to Great*. We found that many of the existing vertical models lacked relevance to classic professions, especially medicine.

We began by interviewing more than 30 physician leaders to attempt to tease a way of determining what the "fault lines" were. We noted that, while many career paths exist in medicine, they follow remarkably similar paths in several important respects: focus of work, relationship to peers, and key strategies for effectiveness. As physicians move phases, they go through a period of uncertainty. This is simply expressed by Marshall Goldsmith in the title of one of his books: *What Got You Here Won't Get You There*. During these periods of uncertainty, the physician must switch strategies. Many doctors who plateau earlier than they would like, or "derail," did not properly adjust their leadership approaches.

The physician leadership model that resulted from our work can be described as "push, then pull." The first phase of physician leadership is about building personal competence, by pushing oneself in some combination of research, clinical practice, and teaching. Simply said, one emerges from Phase I as a capable professional. If done well, especially if accompanied by a reputation for being collegial, a second phase is characterized by the attraction of others in proximity who seek to join the process. This building phase ends in Phase III when the work that you have done begins to bring national and international recognition and the "pull" effect becomes primary. (Many physicians know "push" very well, yet find they have little experience with "pull.") Emerging stars in the field are drawn to you, willing to relocate to join your team. The Phase III leader spends much of his/her time responding to the inquiries about joining his efforts (center, department, etc.). In the fourth phase of development, institutions seek you out as one of only a few who could create a group of international distinction. The fifth and last phase, which only a few may achieve, is when a senior and respected leader proactively disrupts the industry through reinvention. In this case, the physician leader becomes the face of a new and transformative movement.

While, it may seem at first glance that this model is more about career development than leadership per say, it actually tracks increasing **influence** (alternatively defined as social capital), the asset most critical to effective leadership.

When physicians work from this model, they can simultaneously focus on owning their current phase of development while preparing for the next rung of the ladder. The result is a development process that is both effective and efficient and imbues physician leaders with a greater set of tools, insights, and perspectives. Equally important, they can ensure that they do not leave a phase until they have accomplished the key goals within it, learned its most important lessons, and fully readied themselves for the next phase. "Derailing" or early plateauing, often results from people advancing phases before they are ready. With holes in their skill set, even if not in their curriculum vitae, they find they are not being selected for positions or are not emerging as the leaders they had hoped to be.

As a final caveat, we recognize that many people, fully capable of succeeding at the next level as defined by title or administrative responsibility, may choose to remain in an earlier stage. In most situations, this occurs because they understand well that their true passion lies in the activities of each day and the satisfaction it brings them. They may also rightly believe that their work as a researcher, clinician, or teacher benefits society more than any contribution they might make as an

administrator. We deeply respect this paradigm and might argue that, in these instances, their leadership skills are redirected toward their academic or clinical discipline on a national or international level rather than institutional service.

Details of Physician Leadership Model

One metaphor we often use to describe physician leadership development is that of sports. A team sport, in particular, produces many stars but few superstars. Those individuals who receive the most fame and are part of the most successful teams are those who maximize both their talent and their partnership with others, such as Michael Jordan and Scottie Pippen of the 1990s-era Chicago Bulls. Rarer still are the coaches who can create an environment where this level of high-performance results from athletes with larger-than-life egos deciding to work together for a common goal. A few move to roles where they oversee many coaches, as owner of a franchise or commissioner of a sports enterprise. Rarest of all are the individuals who effectively create a "new game," going beyond the limitations of what came before. These pioneers produced the modern versions of baseball, basketball, NASCAR, and every other sport.

Phase I: "Team Player"

Phase I starts when the physician sets out on his or her career after finishing training and residency. Unlike many other professions, the investment of time and effort (and money) to become a doctor is extreme and the newly trained physician has many engrained patterns of behavior, social norms, and talents to draw on. Phase I is about establishing yourself, effectively learning the ropes of clinical practice or research, and creating the base from which future leadership will emerge.

Work focus: Establishing yourself as you also establish strong working relationships.

In a word, you are: Establishing.

Others are: Colleagues.

View of self: A peer.

Affiliation focus: You are well liked.

Aha moment: My reputation is as important as my skills.

Push/pull dominance: Push, to get oneself established and to take ownership of one's reputation.

Key insights: I need to develop myself as well as I can or I will not be credible or respected enough to lead others. Develop the insight that the most important problems require collaboration. While many mid-functioning teams are really one person carrying the load, the greatest innovations result from those units that truly function collaboratively with many contributors.

Credibility threshold to move to the next level: You are seen as a regional leader, respected as much for how you do things as for what you do.

Attitudes that predict early plateau: I am the smartest one around and working with others is overrated. Now, as I get established, I can do what I want. I do not work well with others because others are not up to my level.

Phase II: "Team Captain"

Phase II starts when you are seen as a regional leader (leadership as a measure of influence). The team captain is sought out for mentoring at a local level. In an academic setting, Phase II is usually when a person becomes an associate professor. Phase II is where the emerging leader makes decisions that will guide the rest of his or her career. If you choose the individual contributor route, where your team is visualized as a "star and supporting cast," your leadership ascendancy will plateau. The focus of Phase II is grasping the key concept that helping others is the most important way of helping yourself.

Work focus: Building a reputation by building a team.

In a word, you are: Building.

Others are: Both colleagues and friends.

View of self: Builder of talent.

Affiliation focus: Being respected is the key measure of effectiveness, as your time is invested in helping others as a means to help yourself.

Aha moment: Mentoring is the best way to get what I want.

Push/pull dominance: Push, to get work done and make time for mentoring. Some people are drawn to you for mentoring (pull begins).

Key insights: Mentoring is reciprocal. With others working with me leveraging all our talents, we can reach for national or international goals. What got me to this point is not what will take me to the next level. It is important to not seem overwhelmed around others. I need to handle my own issues and not dump on others.

Credibility threshold to move to the next level: Your reputation becomes national.

Attitudes that predict early plateau: Mentoring is fine, as long as it does not get in the way of what is important (which is my own work and my own career). Junior people do not work as hard/are not as smart as I was at that stage. I try to minimize my contact with others because it is a timesink. The less time I spend with others, the more important work I get done.

Phase III: Coach

Phase III begins as the leader's reputation becomes national or international and others are drawn to the expanding work. For those on the academic road, the title at this point ranges from full professor through chair.

Work focus: Attracting others.

In a word, you are: Integrating.

Others are: Colleagues who could someday allow us to go beyond what we are doing now.

View of self: Creating a place (disease center, practice, etc.) that is big enough to accommodate the stars who want to join us.

Affiliation focus: You want to be liked; you do not need to be liked.

Aha moment: We are famous! Great people are willing to pull up stakes and move here, just to work with us. This is our time to produce; to say what we will do and to do it.

Push/pull dominance: Pull, as people seek you out for help, mentoring, or to join your efforts.

Key insights: How I work is now much more important than what I do. My time is best spent empowering others, as my impact is now measured by what others do. Anything that happens here that is good is their doing; anything that happens here that is bad is my responsibility. "Golf course diplomacy"—working out problems and deepening relationships in a context unrelated to work issues—is a key tool for getting things done.

Credibility threshold to move to the next level: People think about and talk with you about considering the prime jobs in the field.

Attitudes that predict early plateau: This success is the result of what I have done. I am now finally free to call all the shots. I need great people who will do what I say. I get irritated when others claim responsibility for what I have done. Time to maximize what we are already doing, rather than continuing to reach for something new. We are successful enough executing our current business plan that we can ignore what is going on around us.

Phase IV: Team President

Phase IV begins as the leader is sought out for new jobs, often the most prestigious in the field. For those physicians who have followed traditional paths, such as the academic route, the typical role at this point is dean or president.

Work focus: Being attracted to new leadership roles.

In a word, you are: Called (as in, the phone rings).

Others are: Receptive to your leadership.

View of self: Gratitude for opportunities, desire to make this next opportunity really count; an earned humility.

Affiliation focus: You are sought out to make the tough calls and tend to do so through both consensus-building and value-driven decision-making.

Aha moment: The best way to get the right opportunity is to stop auditioning for the part. You will be known for what you do next, more so than everything else up to this point.

Push/pull dominance: Pull, as people try to influence your decisions about where to go and what to do.

Key insights: Your days of doing are over. The needs of your family must be weighed against your career desires. At most you have one or two moves ahead of you. Your reputation now has a momentum, and it is important to run a great operation or this reputation will sour.

Credibility threshold to move to the next level: People begin to talk to you about crazy and disruptive ideas (often focused on emerging technology), and you find yourself considering out-of-the-box career moves.

Attitudes that predict early plateau: It is about time! Of course this should be happening. I am the natural one to lead the top institution in my field.

Phase V: Sports Commissioner (or League Founder)

Phase V beings as the person graduates from traditional career paths to start and/or lead something that produces disruptive change in their field. The literature on entrepreneurship distinguishes between people who start new companies, often with the desire of exiting during an IPO, and those who establish dominant new industries. Founders in sports have created NASCAR, the X Games, extreme sports, etc. Founders have also led the move to create video games based on sports or sports franchises.

Work focus: Disrupting others (as in disruptive change).

In a word, you are: Free to focus on what the future will bring your industry.

Others are: Doing something that will completely change in a few years, and they need to know about it.

View of self: You are doing things that you never thought you would be doing. Every day seems a continuation of your own self-reinvention.

Affiliation focus: You need to get your message across and that happens as much socially as it does in professional settings.

Aha moment: This is really fun! Change does not need to be hard, but it will never be easy.

Push/pull dominance: A combination of both. Push for change, and then pull from the people who are drawn to you. Unlike phases III and IV, there is not always a place to put great people.

Key insights: You are leading change in the industry, but the moment you take yourself too seriously, you lose your effectiveness.

Credibility threshold to move to the next level: There is no phase VI, but there are varying levels of impact within V. You find that your challenge shifts from convincing people to accept something that is counterintuitive to being confronted by others who regard you as a pioneer whose time has passed.

Attitudes that predict early plateau: Unless I am the face of change, it is not change I approve of.

One final comment: while, we have often referenced traditional academic job titles in characterizing the progressive career stages described earlier, it is our strong belief that even in nonacademic models, physicians still find themselves moving up through the phases in the way we have described. Analogous levels of leadership (going from "team player" to "team captain" to "coach" and beyond) can be identified in nearly all healthcare and bioscience organizations.

Chapter 3
Phase I: Team Player

Phase I is a time of extraordinary excitement and satisfaction. You have completed a period of arduous training, and you are anxious to test and demonstrate your skills (to yourself as well as others). Indeed, you may have some degree of insecurity, as you are now effectively unsupervised on a day-to-day basis. Without question, you are personally responsible to a greater level than when in a training program.

At the time commitments and stresses of embarking on independent clinical practice or setting up a laboratory may crowd out an awareness of the need to nurture the personal traits that will set the foundation for your later professional behavior. As most physicians relocate to a different institution after training, the mundane details of establishing a routine for everyday life (finding the best route to work in the morning, which dry cleaner stays open late) can take up too much of your personal bandwidth. These distractions can be dramatically characterized as a tyranny of the urgent over the important.

Moving into a new location or professional role cannot be accomplished without some angst, but there are at least a few strategies that can reliably lessen the load. The first is **developing rational expectations**. This will require engagement with a senior mentor (perhaps your direct superior but not always). As well, you will need to formulate the most objective view you can muster of

B. L. Gewertz, D. C. Logan, *The Best Medicine*,
DOI 10.1007/978-1-4939-2220-8_3,
© Springer Science+Business Media New York 2015

your own prospects. It may be helpful to use Harry Davis' technique (referred to in Chap. 1) of visualizing "what would success look like" in 1, 3, and 5 years. The more specific these goals can be, the more they will guide your efforts. While it is tempting to make specific goals for each area of your endeavors, we have found that limiting them to just a few (three to four at most) is best. After all, those who attain wide recognition in our society usually are known for excellence in one thing.

The next important step is using these validated goals to **set your priorities**. At this stage of your career, you will be presented with a large number of opportunities. Many will be worthwhile but a much smaller number will directly contribute in achieving your key goals. By prioritizing and sticking to it, you will not have to agonize over every conflict of commitment that crops up.

When Bruce moved from his senior resident position at the University of Michigan to an assistant professorship at the University of Texas-Southwestern, he had three key goals—establish a clinical practice, outfit a laboratory for basic physiologic research, and further his interest in undergraduate medical education. The time course of each was different. The day he received clinical privileges, he was allowed to operate. In contrast, surveying available laboratory resources, ordering equipment, and developing collaborations and a research plan would require at least 6–12 months. His priority setting was enhanced by a conversation with a senior academic surgeon who wisely counseled him that "you only have one chance to demonstrate your clinical interest and competence; people are going to make up their mind about those in short order." In contrast, research productivity was judged based on medium to long-term results. He strongly recommended that for the first year, Bruce prioritize his availability for clinical work, allowing the laboratory set-up to move forward at its own pace and putting off taking over the student educational programs for a few years. This clarity reduced uncertainty until Bruce better understood his environment and, in fact, his true interests and capabilities.

It is important to note that this aforementioned counsel does not propose a purely transactional view of personal and professional efforts; i.e., "I will only work on projects that specifically advance my key objectives." There is intense satisfaction and growth in providing institutional service beyond one's specific areas of focus. Others will take note of such unselfish behavior, and it builds your reputation as a team player, which is both admirable and necessary. That said, keeping priorities at the forefront does allow young professionals to clearly define whether core activities would need to be proportionately scaled down to accept other responsibilities. This is generally the point at which limits should be set.

Priority setting cannot be limited to your professional activities. It is critical that you clearly identify the personal commitments of greatest importance to you. While this may seem self-evident, it is our observation that the pattern of reduced autonomy during medical school and residency often makes it difficult for even the most organized and mature young physicians to claim proper control of their own time. After all, your personal responsibility for your patients is hardly lessened by beginning independent practice. Clinical duties will always be beckoning.

It is often useful to think of your career as a marathon not a sprint. Consistent with this metaphor, you need to ensure that the most valuable long-term assets and joys are protected and nurtured. Frequent and thoughtful considerations should be given to your spouse, children, and family. It is equally important that you maintain your own personal health and fitness; indeed, it is frequently observed that many young physicians have no primary doctor, relying on irregular "curbside" consults from their colleagues in lieu of a formal doctor–patient relationship.

Finding balance requires both short-term and long-term accommodations. In the short term, you can make the best efforts to control your calendar by insuring that any meeting or activity is specifically and actively approved before it is scheduled. In doing so, it is also helpful to protect enough free time that you can focus on longer-term projects and/or respond to any unanticipated requirements for your participation. Many of the senior leaders we spoke with set aside up to two half days per week to allow them to properly focus on whatever work was needed but unanticipated. This luxury may be less available to Phase I physicians, but the practice can be modeled by purposely allocating the time required for tasks and not falling into the disquieting circumstance of always feeling that you don't have the freedom to pay proper attention to what needs to be done right. In short order, you will learn that there can't be any compromise on the material that has your name on it.

Needed Skills

We will next consider a number of key attitudes and competences that need to be developed in Phase 1. All of these share one unifying principle. **In order to be authentic and consistently displayed, positive attitudes and behaviors should be based on core values ... and the fewer the better.** In our interviews with senior healthcare executives, nearly all spontaneously mentioned the necessity of putting their organizations' values in the center of any business decisions. To ensure this is the case, they regularly assessed their own behaviors and attitudes to be certain that they *personally* modeled and reinforced the ideals of the organizations they led. Developing such insight was felt to be critical to their success.

While executives described a wide range of detailed business objectives and strategies, when discussions addressed core values, the same three were mentioned time and again—**integrity, collegiality, and accountability.**

Integrity

It is axiomatic that integrity is an essential value. It is equally well accepted that this virtue is by no means uniformly expressed in the current corporate genome. It is widely held that an important driver of our recent economic downturn was a failure of a large number of commercial financial institutions to consistently demonstrate integrity in their strategic and operational activities.

For the young physician in Phase 1, the needed integrity is highly personal not institutional. It is best summarized by the aphorism "your word is your bond." This is not to say that such honorable conduct was not highly valued all along in your personal and professional life but only to acknowledge that the expectation for consistency and honesty is even greater the further one progresses in a career. Importantly, now more people will notice if you fall short. Integrity, like all reputational elements, is very difficult to regain once lost.

It is simply very important that promises made are kept. This can be accomplished by understanding what you personally can deliver and what you can only hope to influence. In the negative, Lyndon Johnson once famously said "Never tell someone to go to hell unless you can send them there!" Similarly, never promise a favorable outcome unless you are the only variable in achieving it. In the executive coaching parlance, it is always better to "under promise and over deliver."

Collegiality

Collegiality is an important skill to nurture at this stage. Solid, responsible personal relationships facilitate the open communications and compromises needed to achieve optimal results in clinical, research, or administrative missions. Collegiality can be furthered by making real efforts to know more about your co-workers independent of their "day job." More than just improving the function of the unit, it is a rewarding aspect of life. As we can all attest, working with people you know, like, and respect is an ideal situation—and well worth all the effort involved to establish such connections. That said, it is both unlikely and impractical that you will be personally close to everyone or that you and all of your colleagues will uniformly desire the same level of familiarity. **An environment of professional collegiality is established not by being a best friend to all but rather by uniformly maintaining a respectful posture to others and an openness to deepening relationships where mutually desired.**

The straightforward goal of being respectful to all can be tested by the daily pressures of clinical medicine or the high level of creativity demanded by cutting-edge research. As much as anything, maintaining collegiality requires being sensitive to others' ruffled feelings and being willing to address conflicts directly and soon. Indeed, it is quite common that long-term personal relationships are strengthened by occasional conflict as long as grievances are not allowed to simmer. The discussion associated with the conflict should be focused on achieving a level of understanding by both parties not settling a perceived injustice.

In these situations, perhaps the best mantra is "you don't have to win every argument." In the day-to-day work setting, very few conflicts are primal ones reflecting character weaknesses or dishonesty. In our interviews, senior leaders repeatedly opined that in their experience the vast majority of disagreements, even serious ones, are driven by reasonable and qualified people holding divergent opinions regarding what's best for the group. In resolving contested issues, nothing is more important than the assumption of good intentions by all parties. Conversely, nothing can poison working relationships more than the predetermination of malevolence. While disruptive and destructive behaviors are certainly seen in every setting, both academic and commercial, the successful leader never assumes the worst in people's behavior.

Most of all, Phase I physician leaders who appreciate and nurture collegiality in their working group enable more imaginative problem solving. Social research in a wide range of endeavors clearly shows that collecting a wide range of opinions offers a better chance at untangling the most complex problems. Notably termed "the wisdom of crowds" by James Surowieki (the title of his famous book), he and others hypothesize that one of the characteristics of truly difficult challenges is the need for the successful integration of many different skill sets and experience to arrive at the optimal, if unconventional, solution.

Achieving balance between collegiality and competitiveness is often a challenge to the young physician leader. It is axiomatic that highly motivated people wish to win and, for much of their life, excellence is too often defined only in comparison with their peers. With progression through Phase I, one's peer group expands across generations and, quite often, previous challengers morph into key collaborators. Hence, competition must be reformatted to become an affirmative, but not consuming, motivational force rather than a rivalry. In this setting, peers effectively push each other to excel by offering inspiration that great new things can be done—both together and singly. It is our observation that those who grasp this nuanced view—what could be called "cooperative competition"—gain great reputational value and make more rapid progress in both their productivity and career path.

Such relationships are perhaps most clearly seen in the creative arts. Van Gogh and Gauguin worked side by side in Arles in 1890, gaining insights from each other that were truly revolutionary. Indeed the evolution of modern art from impressionism to cubism to abstract expressionism was accomplished by groups of talented, if imperfect, people coaching, cajoling and, in the end, inspiring each other.

In his classic book, *Crossing to Safety*, Wallace Stegner beautifully chronicled the life-long relationship of two English professors and their wives who profoundly influenced each other's professional and personal self-images. His autobiographical novel focuses on the difficulties of using a close friend as a measure of achievement without stimulating jealousy. The narrator realizes that life, with its challenges, victories, and defeats, can only be enjoyed with the close company of others travelling the same path who may, at times, be rivals for jobs or recognition.

This proper balance of collegiality and competition is well illustrated by the difference in attitude between people who say "I am competing with talented people; I must constantly monitor their productivity and exceed it" and those who say "I am honored to be in the company of talented people; their excellence will inspire me to be the best I can be."

Accountability

Accountability is a third key value along with integrity and collegiality. In Phase I, accountability is personal not organizational. It is truly a learned skill, as when something goes wrong, too often our first instincts are to look toward someone else's performance as a cause. An important indicator of maturation into a professional is overcoming this predisposition.

Modeling personal accountability is aided by the realization that, irrespective of the qualifications of workers and their quality of work, all organizations experience difficulties. As physicians, who are trained to be prepared for complications of diseases or treatments, we should understand that the differentiation between good and bad performance is usually the relative incidence of problems not the elimination of them. In most situations, long-term judgments of our performance or character usually focus on how we deal with problems. Acknowledging that it is *your problem* irrespective of cause and focusing your efforts on "fixing things rather than fixing the blame" will lead to more durable solutions. Co-workers, above and below you in the hierarchy, will recognize your emphasis on getting things right the next time and not dwelling in the past.

This tenet does not excuse a consistently bad track record or the "normative error," which reflects unacceptable and often unethical behavior (dishonesty or criminal behavior). Rather, it is the realization that the essence of leadership of small groups is dealing effectively with intermittent shortcomings in function or personnel. A number of leaders we talked to quipped, "that's why they pay me the big bucks."

Beyond understanding and displaying favorable traits, it is important that young physicians develop consistency in these interpersonal behaviors. Physicians are drilled during residency training to attain this type of uniformity in clinical practice or research protocols but, too often, consistency in relationships with peers is inadequately emphasized and, hence, not internalized. Indeed, overall consistency of performance is a final and critical quality of successful Phase 1 leaders. It is can be summed up by the simple statement that "pros play hard every game."

Chapter 4
Phase II: Team Captain

In Phase II, your day-to-day activities—clinical care, research, administration—may not substantially change from Phase I. You are already established as an independent professional. You have enjoyed some success and gained recognition, perhaps even nationally. The key motivation of Phase II is the appreciation that sustaining this high level of performance as your professional work matures will require a larger platform with more resources.

You can rightly point to your initial accomplishments to aid you in negotiating additional assets. That said, institutional leaders would be more likely persuaded to invest in your projects if they get the sense that such investments will benefit more than your narrow self-interest. In short, they will want to be convinced that your future successes will enrich the organization more broadly. This can be best accomplished by demonstrating that your reputation for collegiality can be leveraged to attract and develop top talent within the organization.

The biggest shift from Phase I to II may be in mindset and how to determine success. Phase I success is most often about the "what"—results. In Phase II, the results are still important, but the "how" those outcomes are achieved becomes equally important. Many physician leaders we interviewed noted that this

B. L. Gewertz, D. C. Logan, *The Best Medicine,*
DOI 10.1007/978-1-4939-2220-8_4,
© Springer Science+Business Media New York 2015

shift is obvious years or decades after the transition to Phase II, but was rarely apparent at the time.

A new assistant medical director we interviewed—someone just moving into Phase II—noted that her instructions upon hiring were to "fix the front" of the emergency department, which she said consists of triage, registration and flow. She described the first few days of her new job as "testing the waters," and learning about specific people's agendas, adding that "what made me successful before is not exactly what I now needed to do, and it was a little disorienting."

Needed Skills

The knack of inspiring others to coalesce and work together can be referred to as "stickiness." The metaphor implies that your persona binds together co-workers with varied skill sets. Most likely, these people will be diverse both in personality and how they go about their work. Think of the differences in the general methods and personalities of engineers versus those of salesman. To unite such different styles your behaviors will need to be, in one word, inclusive.

> **"I'm not arguing, I'm simply explaining why I am right!"**

Achieving this goal will likely require "cooling" your own advocacy at times to give others a chance to innovate and lead. After all, you wish to assemble a team of leaders. While this needs to be implemented at a strategic level, it is often most clearly seen in the way a developing leader approaches daily discussions. A simple metric is noting how much of the "air time" in any given meeting you are taking up. For example, if you are meeting with three others, do you talk more or less than 25 % of the time? Further, do you find yourself falling into the trap of interrupting someone else's explanation to rebut facts or argue your position rather than reserving your comments for later? It is perfectly appropriate to set the stage and define objectives for a meeting, but rarely useful to be the first to offer an opinion on the outcome.

It is generally accepted that empowering all qualified people to input into a decision increases the value of the process. It also is one of the most powerful means to reinforce participants' feelings of self-worth and validity.

A large number of the senior executives with whom we spoke mentioned the importance of the "local rules" by which their meetings are conducted. They emphasized that the commitment to allow all to express their views was an unwritten but deeply imprinted part of their corporate culture. Another pragmatic benefit of allowing others to speak first is the real possibility that, even without your input, they will endorse the same position or action that you might have advocated. By accepting their conclusion, you give them a strong sense of ownership—even if you may consider it your idea.

Whether in a formal meeting or a chance encounter, the key to becoming "sticky" is making others feel better about themselves for having interacted with you. While you can occasionally accomplish this by providing them with something tangible— a new grant, a raise—fate usually does not allow that to happen repeatedly. Rather, the gift you can bestow on every interaction, without cost, is your personal endorsement of someone's value to you. This can be as simple as a kind word or smile.

Restating this key principle—you should evaluate your interactions by whether it elevates the other person's view of themselves, not by whether she perceives you in a more positive light. If you accomplish the former, the latter will reliably follow.

Paying attention to these personal interactions and not letting short-term frustrations influence your social behavior is a critical leadership skill at any level. What happened 10 min ago cannot be allowed to put a negative spin on your other relationships, especially with those who have nothing to do with the issue. As we all know, most of these daily details and disagreements will be forgotten in short order, as they are resolved in their time. What can linger—well beyond the life span of any given conflict—are the hard feelings engendered by antagonistic personal behavior.

The aforementioned advice does not imply that you can or should fundamentally change your personal traits. **To be consistent and credible, your behavior must be based on your "true self."** If you are introverted, it is not necessary or recommended that you morph into the most outgoing person at every social occasion. What is needed is for you to spend some effort to identify and augment the ways in which *you* feel comfortable interfacing with your peers in a positive manner. You will simply not be as successful if you cannot find a personal style that allows regular and appropriate acknowledgment of the value of your peers. For example, it is possible that an appreciative note or email is more aligned with your personality than a spontaneous hallway chat. An invitation to meet for coffee may work better for you than a scheduled appointment in your office. As soon as your methods are recognized as being genuine and consistent with past behavior, your colleagues will be attuned to your affirming actions.

Despite our hopes, personal or working relationships are not always positive. Even excellent relationships, with longstanding value, go through turbulent periods. In most cases, corrective actions can resolve the difference or, at worst, allow for thoughtful realignment to the benefit of both parties. The most important attributes of such conflict resolution are learned during Phase II when, often for the first time, the young professional is managing a number of people.

One of the keys to conflict resolution is employing a direct approach. Whenever possible, you should seek to discuss the disagreement in private. It is desirable to do so in a timely manner but certainly not in moments of stress, if it can be avoided. It is important that you not discuss issues with any third parties before talking to the person with whom you are at odds. Although such venting can feel therapeutic in the short-term, publicizing your troubles only associates you with conflict and nothing much good can come from it. If you subsequently resolve the issue, obviously no one needed to know. If the other side hears details of the dispute (often wrong) through back channels, they will be strongly inclined to broadcast their side of the story in defense. This ends up being injurious to both of your reputations and commonly interferes with what could be a positive resolution. In our experience, nothing can impair a favorable outcome more than a disagreement between peers gaining the stature of a "feud."

In working through disagreements between peers, it is often useful to determine whether the alternative views reflect a different set of facts, a different interpretation of facts or, most seriously, a fundamental conflict of values. Senator Daniel Patrick Moynihan observed that "everyone is entitled to their own opinion but not their own facts." Clearly articulating an approach that allows both of you to work through these determinations in a stepwise fashion can help create a more comfortable atmosphere for both parties.

These discussions can be usually be simply structured in three steps:

- Deliberate what facts are available and what additional information needs to be gathered,
- Outline specific areas of agreements and differences,
- Search for solutions.

On occasion a discrete third-party, trusted by both but impartial to the topic at issue, can help set a collegial tone. Interestingly, Phase III leaders commonly are called upon to play this role, which is not so much a mediator as a facilitator. We will deal more with this in later chapters.

Further Establishing Your Brand

Perhaps for the first time, you have a chance to establish the type of environment you and your team work in. **Your priority should be setting clear norms for interpersonal behaviors by ensuring that your words and deeds reinforce those local values that you all share.** That said, this will require a fairly high level of tolerance for individual styles or even real eccentricities as long as these behaviors do not compromise the overall work atmosphere or conflict with core values.

A well-known example of these leadership skills can be seen in the coaching style of basketball's Phil Jackson. In both Chicago and Los Angeles, he was gifted with superstar athletes (Michael Jordon and Kobe Bryant). That said, he attributed his success not so much to modifying their attitudes (although there was important work done with them) but to establishing a way of doing business that allowed all on the team to contribute and excel to the best of their abilities. The key value was the expectation that the coaching staff was going to provide the customized mentorship for each player that allowed them to both improve their skill set and to function better within the system.

Succeeding to the extent Phil Jackson did (11 championships in two very different environments) was dependent on blending different types of personalities and talents over relatively long time. This clearly mandated in an environment with consistent values and codes of behavior. Although there are obviously many differences between professional athletes and physicians, the group sizes assembled by most Phase II leaders are similar in number (15–20) to the number of players and support staff of a basketball team. Further, both groups have self-evident goals: winning NBA championships or providing exemplary patient care, research discoveries and teaching. **Hence, the thing that distinguishes exceptional groups in sports or medicine is not the mission but the methods. It is our contention that acquiring the skills needed to mentor co-workers—offering them opportunities to become better at what they do—is the single most important characteristic of successful Phase II leaders.** As their reputation for developing others grows, they are able to attract the most highly motivated people and inspire better performance from them.

One of the characteristics of productive mentor–mentee relationships is that they are mutually desired. It is not rational to force someone into either role; in this regard, mentorship is distinctly different from "reporting relationships" which can, in fact, be mandated.

When a junior colleague seeks you out for advice or support, it is the best reflection of multiple positive elements of your reputation. In the main, you are perceived as being:

- Successful and upwardly mobile.
- Empathetic and accessible.
- Savvy and politically insightful.

As much as any indicator, being valued as a mentor is perhaps the best indication that your leadership potential has been noted within the organization.

Knowing When to Share Personal and Professional Confidences

In Phase II leadership positions, you will have less experienced physicians and other professionals working directly for you, perhaps for the first time. In doing so, many of your laudable behaviors toward others will need to become even more refined. For one, being true to your personal commitments (an essential element for sure) is necessary but not sufficient in Phase II. **You will also have to demonstrate a uniform capacity to keep confidences**.

From time to time, you will be entrusted with knowledge of a wide range of private matters. Indeed, it is a marker of your growing stature and reputation that your co-workers, mentees, and even your superiors trust you with their feelings and concerns. Your stewardship of these "secrets" must be absolute, as violation of their trust can never be successfully remedied.

We all know otherwise capable people whose advancement has been limited by their poor guardianship of such confidences. It is a particularly virulent affliction for anyone's reputation and can spread rapidly through the organization and even beyond. When they disclose the sensitive information to a third-party, the recipient may or may not be interested, but one thing is certain they will never make the mistake of sharing any of their private information with the culprit and will certainly not seek them out for advice.

They Do Not Call It "Middle Management" for Nothing!

You will have to develop other skills to manage "up" and "down" the hierarchy. **In Phase I your level of accountability was personal. In Phase II, it becomes more institutional.** As a consequence of your growing stature within the organization, you will be expected to pitch in vigorously to address shortcomings beyond your sphere of influence. This expectation is driven principally by your value as a role model to all. Further, few things will gain more positive notice from the leadership levels above you than your personal commitment to the overall mission.

One senior executive we spoke to described his remarkable "battlefield promotion" from a mid-level faculty member to the most senior executive of an academic medical center. While this rapid rise was doubtless a reflection of his extraordinary personal skill set and strong record, he also attributed it to the simple co-incidence of his resolving a pesky "town-gown" issue within the community. To his good fortune, this very visible bit of diplomacy occurred just as a sudden vacancy developed in the office of executive vice president (VP) and dean. Because of his collaborative style and willingness to step into and solve a problem beyond his parochial interests, he was viewed as viable leader who, despite his relative inexperience, could well represent the institution's interests.

Hiring And Firing

You doubtless have developed insights into how to properly motivate groups and maintain team performance during your training. The nature of group leadership changes during Phase II. In particular, you will have a greater role in selection, on-going performance review, and promotion or termination of professionals and staff.

Perhaps for the first time, you will have an opportunity to pick the people who work directly with you. Although nothing is more important to your success than such personnel decisions, most physicians are not well versed on the basics of candidate interviewing and selection. Indeed, highly experienced executives in all fields freely admit to biases and misjudgments no matter how focused they are on the process. Even the most promising recruitments may not yield a long-term employment relationship; some estimate at least a 25 % failure rate with all the pain and costs of separation and retraining next hire.

There are a few practices that can improve your batting average. It is important to involve a wide range of people in the initial vetting and interview process. While it may seem obvious that this group should include, in particular, those who will be working most closely with the new hire, it is remarkable how frequently this is not achieved. On other occasions, the input of co-workers is not sufficiently heard. The most effective method to properly evaluate a potential recruit is to get feedback in private from each interviewee rather than convening a meeting in which one powerful voice can skew the conversation. Such a group discussion is, of course, desirable to facilitate consensus on a final decision but usually should be postponed until all candidates have been interviewed and references checked.

One of the most difficult elements of hiring co-workers or staff is properly assessing your own strengths and weaknesses and matching the new hire's attributes to what you or others in your group cannot easily provide. The trick is finding those people with different skill sets, who frequently may be equally different in style or attitude, and insuring that their integration into the group will not be too disruptive. While the benefits of such recruitments are often worth it, one should not underinvest in the time and effort required to blend talents.

Another key element of selection should be your assessment of what will be needed in the future not just what has worked in the past. We can all acknowledge that when we lose a particularly effective co-worker, our first instinct is to look for someone exactly like them with similar background and skills. This reaction is understandable but, in fact, every vacancy should prompt a fresh evaluation of the role and whether a new skill set or personality might be desirable to meet future needs.

Recently, a chair needed to replace an excellent department director who was promoted to hospital VP. Both of the final two candidates were first rate. One was an accomplished administrator with 12 years experience running nursing and physician practices; her resume and style closely matched the incumbent. The second candidate was a recently minted MBA who had 6 years experience in the workforce as a healthcare consultant and grant administrator. She had limited clinical exposure and no practice management experience. The opinion of the leadership of the department (all of whom met both candidates, often more than once) was split although all agreed both were outstanding. In the end, consensus was reached that the developing changes in medicine favored those who could think "outside the box" and that what worked in the past might very well not work so well in the future. In this scenario, someone who was comfortable in changing environments and who could potentially bring a different perspective was the better choice. Candidate number 2 (with a history of consulting) got the job and the strengths of the director's office moved from practice administration to analysis and strategic planning. Although the director was still responsible for the workings of the clinics and professional revenue stream (and was strongly supported in gaining the skills to do so), the daily administrative load was subtly shifted toward the capable managers who reported to her. In this fashion, the recruitment process was used to re-evaluate the job's priorities and reposition the department's talent for future challenges.

Contrast the aforementioned scenario, another search for a medical administrator is outlined below. Although the leader involved was a Dean/VP (properly Phase IV in our classification), the lessons apply equally well to any leadership role.

The newly arrived Dean was interested in hiring a new practice plan director. He identified a single external candidate who had worked with him at a previous job in a different capacity. The candidate was brought in for interviews but clearly indicated to those he met that the job (unaccompanied by a clear job description) was his to take or not. Shortly after his visit, the Dean/VP gathered the chairs together and asked for their opinions. Several in the room had not met the candidate and may well have wondered why they were excluded from doing so. The first issue the chairs raised was why no job description had been generated for a position that would be a new one for the institution and would doubtless have implications for all departments. When the discussion was finally directed toward the suitability of the candidate, many mentioned the lack of a normal search process and asked why there were no other candidates if the position was so critical to the future. In frustration, the Dean/VP announced that the chairs "were wrong" and that he would do what was "best." This ended up being the immediate hiring of the candidate. Not surprisingly, his reception was not warm and, despite his clear abilities, it took him years to gain the respect and trust he might have been accorded much earlier if his selection had the elements of proper process. Equally unfortunately, the Dean/VP lost some personal credibility with his colleagues even though, in hindsight, most agreed that the practice plan director was a competent and useful addition.

Dealing with Performance Problems

In Phase II, you will be responsible for establishing clear expectations for a wide range of co-workers; this group will likely include many specialists who may have different expertise and experiences. The professionals you supervise will understand that the responsibility for setting institutional goals is not theirs alone. Still, they will greatly appreciate a high level of autonomy at *how* they do their job to accomplish those goals.

Your regular individual meetings with co-workers should focus on both the progress you all are making and theirs assessment of how effective their tactics and styles have been. Separating the two allows you to give helpful feedback on their work behaviors independent of their achievements. If properly implemented, this tactic can allow you to mediate the all too common scenario of the misbehaving employee who gets great results but makes everyone else either miserable or inconvenienced in the process. As we have all experienced, the objective successes of such high performers oft makes us disinclined to give them the proper counseling for their less productive personal interactions.

A director of a cardiac catheterization laboratory recalled a difficult situation with a highly talented cardiologist who was nationally known for his innovative approaches to treating heart disease. Unfortunately, he was equally well known locally for his tardiness and complete disinterest in the efficient function of the laboratory. Indeed, his personal behavior made it virtually impossible to hold anyone who worked in the lab to any reasonable expectations of resource utilization or on-time performance. The lab director instituted a monthly meeting with the high volume cardiologist and several other senior colleagues. They reviewed the laboratory productivity, overtime use, and materials cost. They also "blindly" went over the "physician related" delays in case start and any complaints by referring physicians or technicians regarding the function of the lab. After the third meeting, the physician in question sought out the lab director to get additional information about the identity of the physician most often cited. Not surprisingly, the revelation led to a lengthy discussion, which was aided in its productivity by the fact that it was initiated by the doctor himself. The laboratory director deftly accomplished his first mission—getting the problematic physician to acknowledge his behavior—and was later able to effectively counsel and modify the behavior without rancor.

When colleagues or staff straight-out underperform, you need to both document and communicate your assessment in a timely fashion to the individual involved. Such counseling should be done with utmost discretion. That said, no matter how private your discussions, it is probable that your handling of the situation will be carefully noted by others in the work group. After all, they are likely as aware of the shortcomings of the individual's work as you are.

Their opinion of you as a leader will be shaped by two apparently contradictory elements; first, your willingness to tackle the issue directly and second, whether your actions are perceived as fair. As it is mandatory that the confidentiality of the process be uniformly maintained, the outcome of the intervention will have to speak for itself.

One of the leaders we interviewed (a division chief of gastroenterology) described a situation in which he noted decreased productivity by a previously effective physician. After gathering a timeline of the physician's work product, he met with him and reviewed the data. While the physician involved was initially upset, at subsequent meetings he shared a personal issue that was affecting his energy and interest. Although the situation (an upcoming divorce) was not amenable to any specific remediation, clearing the air allowed the division chief to adjust his colleague's work load for a limited period, giving him the time to deal with the changes in his family and personal life. After 3 months, he returned to full duty. Without any public discussion, the division chief earned considerable esteem among his colleagues for both his honest assessment of the physician's performance and the reasonable and time-limited accommodation that was reached.

Chapter 5
Phase III: Coach

Based on your strong performance, you are now being approached to move up to more influential leadership positions, in your organization or outside it. Phase III jobs give you a chance to recruit and develop talented personnel and to provide a greater level of strategic leadership within a larger organization. While you have been able to pick your closest associates in Phase II, now you have the opportunity to actually create a working environment for others consonant with your ideals. While these opportunities are clearly a validation of your professional work to date, it is equally likely that the interest reflects your personal reputation as someone who interacts well with others. In your career to date, you have matured in your ability to relate productively to others, while establishing yourself as an authority in your field. To achieve success in this next phase, the elements collectively called "emotional intelligence" will require the same serious attention that you mustered to refine your laboratory or clinical skills.

As your success at this next level will be determined by the achievements of others, you should spend more time on empowering and supporting them than augmenting your already considerable academic or clinical accomplishments. This requires a redirection of your own goals and your ego. In this mission, you will need to consciously develop stronger skills of self-appraisal and self-regulation.

B. L. Gewertz, D. C. Logan, *The Best Medicine,*
DOI 10.1007/978-1-4939-2220-8_5,
© Springer Science+Business Media New York 2015

As you take your new position, it is essential that you spend time and effort considering what atmosphere you wish to create and what legacy you hope to leave. Using the metaphor of a swiftly moving boat, Henry Cloud likens the result of one's behavior to a trailing "wake" in the water. Certainly, we all know co-workers and leaders who leave turbulence behind them whereas others are able to move swiftly and decisively with little turmoil and disruption.

To properly evaluate your "wake," you must pay more attention to the effect you have on others, with particular attention to outcomes that are unintended. Few of us are spontaneously gifted with these sophisticated skills of self-appraisal. You need to consciously work at developing the ability to evaluate your effectiveness as you go, in a clear-headed manner. You can then thoughtfully modify your next interaction informed by past experience.

Being able to dispassionately view your performance in real time and, if appropriate, admit you could have done better is not always easy. Yet, there are certainly parallels to this iterative process in the practice of medicine. When one crusty old surgeon was asked how he had developed such good operative judgment he answered, "experience." When asked how you get such experience, he quickly responded "poor judgment."

Understanding Your Needs and Those of Others

After meeting their basic needs for food, clothing, and shelter, most humans want to be liked by others. This is especially true among those aspiring to leadership positions. The further we move along in life however, the more we realize that it is unlikely that this ideal of uniform affection can be attained. As well said by the iconic baseball manager Casey Stengel, "You can't make everyone happy—with their job or you."

> **"I want to be liked but I don't need to be liked."**

Given this reality, it is clear that leaders need to work toward group goals without an excessive focus on the short-term approval of others. This surely does not mean disregarding the input of your colleagues and staff. Not only do they often have exactly the insights you need, but their cooperation and support is essential to the group's success. That said, achieving success will often require disturbing the *status quo* in ways that will make some, if not all, uncomfortable.

In our interviews with a number of Phase III leaders, many remarked that transparency is the best antidote to the disquiet that often accompanies change. Data sharing should include both the facts of the situation as well as the planned interventions, even if the actions will be particularly unpopular with some of the group. It is preferred to have the first discussions in more public forums such that everyone feels engaged. If need be, those that are inclined can challenge the data. Early in the process, it is critical to create an environment of genuine openness to facilitate thoughtful questioning of the assumptions. After all, if the facts are incorrect any solution arising from them is suspect. Having a mid-level executive or outside authority present the information, rather than the group leader, can lessen intimidation and improve feedback. Repetition is useful; the more serious the adaptive challenge is, the more times it should be discussed. It is particularly helpful to benchmark the local problem to similar challenges facing comparable institutions.

In contrast to the open dialogue about the facts, crafting solutions is best done in private before any public disclosure, especially when the actions represent "bad news" for those who may need to make sacrifices. It gives the affected parties a chance to respond and even argue things out without appearing disloyal. Even more importantly, it allows them the opportunity to graciously accept the proposed action and gain institutional and personal credit. Indeed, if those most disadvantaged in the short term can be convinced that the actions are for the overall good, they can serve as the most credible advocates for general acceptance.

A Vice-Dean was faced with a serious long-term shortfall in funding for graduate medical education (GME). The total number of residents would need to be capped even as new initiatives in primary care and other needed specialties were expanding. It was clear that there would be "winners" and "losers" with some training programs shrinking.

A process was developed. It began with a "blue ribbon panel" of 10 medical center leaders to include the chief financial officer, other Deans, chairs, and a range of practitioners involved in education. An outside consultant was retained to lead the small group discussion. Much of the work involved assessment of the national trends in GME funding and the role of GME in the strategic plan of the institution. When general agreement on the facts was reached, an off-site "all hands" meeting was convened including all chairs, residency program directors, and coordinators. The discussion was facilitated by the consultant who had by now become familiar with the institution, the local situation, and many of the people involved. A wide ranging set of solutions were debated.

The "blue ribbon" panel reassembled to consider the options raised by the larger group. They crafted both a strategic plan for GME allocations in the future and outlined the short-term reductions that needed to be made in three programs. The Vice-Dean met immediately and in private with the involved chairs and explained both the rationale and the magnitude of the reduction. The departments experiencing reductions acknowledged the need to trim training slots and agreed to do so if they could not identify other sources of funds. When the plan was discussed amongst all chairs, they did not dissent from acceptance of both the long-term strategy and short-term cuts.

The Vice-Dean attributed the smooth adaptation of the plan to the cooperative nature of his colleagues but also noted the importance of clearly tying an administrative action to a broader strategic plan vetted by a larger group of involved and informed people. This is especially true when there are real adverse consequences for some.

Establishing a Reputation

Whether you are well known to your colleagues or they are recent acquaintances, your co-workers will begin making judgments of your character in short order. The good news is that most are predisposed favorably to new leaders; they simply need some time and positive experiences to develop confidence in you.

As much as possible, you should make time for one-on-one meetings with key personnel. A common mistake is to come to meetings with rigid views or other preconceptions of an individual's attitudes or commitment. If you are new to an institution, ask for their views of the past. If you have a history with person which is less than harmonious, it is often useful to explicitly "wipe the slate clean" and look for ways to demonstrate the sincerity of your approach. This could take the form of an administrative appointment or other public recognition.

In Phase III roles, your personal style becomes more widely known and is a major element of how you are viewed. Your daily interactions now extend well beyond colleagues with similar interests, training, and experience. On a daily basis you interface with other departments or divisions, often with different measures of success (e.g. purely academic vs. some combination of clinical and research goals) or totally dissimilar orientations (unionized employees). The adaptive challenge for Phase III leaders is finding a style compatible with their intrinsic nature that "plays across" these boundaries. Except in rare cases, it is not necessary or desirable that you fundamentally change your public persona only that you make an effort to avoid behaviors that impede collegiality and trust. Sustaining a sincere interest in the opinions of others works toward this goal whether you are an introvert or extrovert.

The ability to actively listen to others is a prized characteristic of successful leaders. Despite the best of intentions, miscommunications are common. One of the best and simplest ways to insure that you have received the message is by ending conversations with something like "from our discussion, this is what I heard." Being explicit in this fashion can lessen those major misunderstanding that can be particularly wounding ("I specifically advised against this but she did it anyway"). Another worthwhile technique is to take notes whenever possible. As your responsibilities increase, along with your age, it is remarkable how often nuances or even critical points are dropped from your memory. As mentioned previously, it is useful to studiously avoid monopolizing the "air space" in any meeting.

The Importance of Consistency

A key characteristic of successful leaders is consistency. This does not mean that we all do not have days in which we are more or less cheerful than others. Consistency refers more to the core values and behaviors that we would all aspire to—fairness, equanimity under duress, civility. These traits are often tested most severely when leaders are confronted with bad news and there is a tendency to project the negativity we feel onto the messenger. This can deter her or others from coming forward with important if disturbing information in the future. As well, it can permanently impair the relationship.

The need to be even-handed is greatest when it appears that the person bringing the news is in part responsible for the problem. Even the best employees will make misjudgments or other errors on occasion. Further, you will need to be unencumbered by emotional turmoil in order to be most effective at fixing what needs to be fixed. While healthy organizations surely monitor the incidence of such mistakes, they also realize that avoiding reflexive retribution encourages prompt reporting of problems.

We spoke to a surgical leader about avoiding recriminations. He recalled his experiences when called into the operating room to help another surgeon address a technical error that resulted in injury to the blood vessels and serious bleeding. The primary surgeon was wise to call for assistance, as he was frustrated by both the occurrence of the iatrogenic injury and his inability to quickly fix it. In contrast, the consulting surgeon was emotionally neutral and saw it properly as a simple laceration, requiring step-wise vascular control and repair.

After thinking this through, he adapted a similar approach when confronted with unanticipated administrative problems. He found that purposefully damping his emotional response enhanced his ability to address the issues involved. After all, getting angry and impatient would be highly unlikely to make anyone feel more comfortable with his subsequent actions. As he said, "in general, the more time we waste figuring out whose fault it is, the less time to spend fixing it."

Consistency is likewise important in your personal relationships with co-workers. This comes into focus when you have a close personal relationship with a colleague who reports to you. Such relationships are both inevitable and desirable, as we generally work with people who share our interests and personalities. Depriving yourself of these meaningful interactions is not a rational option. That said, both parties in the relationship need to respect the boundaries involved. You should not discuss sensitive personnel problems after a racquetball game nor should your friend expect any inside information not available to others. As much as possible, your interactions with your friend at work should parallel those that you have with other colleagues in consistent fashion. Failure to find this balance can lead to demoralization and charges of favoritism.

Managing Disruptive People

Despite the general tendency of most people to instinctively back their leaders, in any large group there will invariably be some that feel less supportive. Their lack of enthusiasm may be manifest by a lack of effort or other passive-aggressive behaviors. On occasion, more overtly hostile actions may occur. These can include actively organizing resistance or sending letters of "no confidence" to more senior leadership.

> **"A manager's job is keeping the 4 guys who hate you away from the 20 who have no opinion."**
> **Casey Stengel**

Dealing with both sets of behaviors may require slightly different tactics, but the principle is the same—**it is just plain unwise to over-react to passive-aggressive actions or, worse yet, respond in a like manner to personal attacks**. Indeed, restraint in these situations is one of the most important elements of emotional intelligence and is termed self-regulation. Developing this level of control is easier if you realize that in the vast majority of instances the ire is, in fact, directed at your *position* not your *person*. Admittedly, in the heat of the moment, this attitude can be difficult to master but the end results, not your emotions, should dictate how you proceed. From long experience, most leaders learn that "taking the bait" and acting uncivilly or hostile, especially in public, will too often equate you with the attacker and will be far more damaging to your reputation than anything already said. You will also be demonstrating that you are overly sensitive to criticism and, at worst, insecure in your convictions and unsure of the support of your superiors.

This strategy need not mean inaction. When the complaints are publicized or sent directly to those to whom you report, it is usually wise to provide your supervisors with a thorough description of the individuals involved and your analysis of the circumstances. If warranted, a data-driven refutation of the complaints in private is appropriate, but any such comments should be delivered in a professional and unemotional tone. Your ability to persevere without losing your perspective or your temper will often enhance your reputation with those above you far more than unjustified criticism will dampen it. It is the rare leader who has not had such an experience; this surely applies to those above you.

A senior chair with more than 20 years of experience described events early in his tenure. An anonymous letter was mailed to the Dean and University Board of Trustees. It was also distributed to many members of the faculty. The letter specifically criticized the chair selection process and the qualifications of the chair-elect. Other departmental leaders appointed by the new chair were also demeaned with a number of personal attacks. By happenstance the new chair was on vacation when this occurred and was unaware of the letter. When he returned one week later, the content of the letter was common knowledge.

In a subsequent meeting with the Dean, the young chair expressed his concern that his departmental leaders would feel unsupported if he took no action on their behalf. He proposed sending a letter to all faculties defending them. The Dean made it clear that neither he nor the Board of Trustees paid any attention to an anonymous and unfounded letter. He encouraged the chair to resist the need to publicly refute anything and offered to meet in private with the department leadership to reassure them of the administration's support for all of them.

After consideration, the chair decided he could best deliver that message himself and did so in a regularly scheduled meeting. The departmental leaders were reassured. The defamatory comments about all of them were quickly forgotten and all served in their positions for years. Indeed, even 20 years later, the chair believed that the decisions to avoid public comment and deliver a measured and discrete response in his own time were the most important decisions of his long running chairmanship.

Creating Time and Space

The demands of Phase III jobs are different from those associated with early and mid-career positions and can cast a long shadow over your leisure and family time. The number of people you supervise is larger, and their interactions become a greater concern. You are interfacing with a broader constituency within and outside your organization. By design, other people's problems become yours. **It is vitally important that you find a way to mitigate the stressors; after all, your equanimity and good judgment are two indispensable assets for your performance in a senior administrative job.**

With thoughtful conduct you can maintain the "down time" needed to re-invigorate yourself. **Part of the process is intellectual and is focused on developing realistic attitudes toward your work.** Assuming a longer-term view of problems may not be easy, but it is essential to successfully coexist with a high-pressure job. As simply stated by many Phase III leaders, their lives improved dramatically when they stopped viewing every problem as an existential threat. If you are perceptive, this becomes easier with increasing time on the job.

Lowering stress can also be addressed by purposefully developing new behaviors based on experience. Understanding the "ebb and flow" of your specific job is critical. For example, budgeting periods are generally stressful and you can expect to feel tense during this time. You should plan for that reality and wisely restrict travel and other commitments so that you can be engaged in the process without undue time pressure.

Another wearing component of Phase III jobs is the continuous high level of responsibility. Given your position in the hierarchy, it is not likely you can or should limit your availability for time-sensitive strategic discussions. That said, it is not unreasonable to restrict the amount of personal time you spend on less urgent matters. This needs to be done in a manner sensitive to the needs of your colleagues and staff. There are doubtless times where their emotions can elevate otherwise routine issues to major concerns. In these instances, they may need reassurance and support sooner rather than later.

This can be accomplished by demonstrating to your colleagues that you are, in fact, uniformly accessible for urgent matters. When contacted, you can evaluate whether this is an actual catastrophe needing immediate action (a very small minority of times) or something less. In the main, you can address their concerns relatively quickly by acknowledging your receipt of the information and providing a firm timetable for further discussion and resolution of the issues involved. Putting forward a concrete schedule with specific endpoints will relieve most anxieties and allow proper scheduling of your participation in the process.

Sharing the Load

Just as you have learned to delegate operational responsibilities to others within your unit, it is also advantageous to share the weight of major strategic decisions with them. When a new leader realizes that her senior colleagues have just as strong an interest in their mutual success as she does, the personal burden is lessened.

When Bruce was serving as chair of surgery at the University of Chicago, he encountered a very significant budgetary challenge. Because of the unfavorable malpractice climate in Cook County, the underwriters recommended that the self-insurance pool for medical liability be substantially increased. Overnight, the required departmental contribution increased from $4 to $12 million.

At this level, liability coverage was slated to represent 25% of the overall expenses of the department. During budget negotiations, Bruce was frustrated and anxious and unable to posit a reasonable solution. Weekends offered no respite as a deadline approached.

One sleepless night, he wondered who else was so vitally interested in the problem that they might have creative ideas to contribute to the resolution. He realized that his section leaders were undoubtedly so motivated. During the next week, he organized a series of meeting with the section leaders. The group went through a series of options and, in the end, the department made a number of significant expense reductions (amounting to approximately one-third of the increased cost) and proposed sharing the remaining expense with the hospital and University. The fact that the department offered substantial cost reductions up front was a strong sign of good faith and unity and contributed to the adoption of the plan by all entities.

Many of the other leaders we spoke to related similar stories early in their tenures. They all noted that the tendency to keep problems sequestered and unshared with others who have legitimate and vital interests was neither good leadership nor personally sustaining.

There are some times when a leader should be less inclined to share issues with their senior colleagues. The most obvious circumstance is when a problem is unlikely to affect them. As an institutional leader, many issues beyond those impacting your division will be revealed to you. Even if they are not highly confidential, it is probably not in your interest to be the one circulating the information unless specifically directed to do so.

Know When to be Flexible

Even the most successful ventures encounter serious obstacles and suffer reversals at times. Whether in business or in medicine, when confronted with adversity you must demonstrate confidence in your planning and soldier on. That said, it is critical that your commitment should be to your goals and values, not to any specific operational plan. While it would not be appropriate to abandon a well-designed strategy at the first sign of trouble, a key ability of a leader is the ability to adapt tactics to circumstances without compromising long-term objectives.

> **"It is important to be doggedly determined but don't be an ostrich."**
>
> **Frank Litwak**

Objective midcourse reviews of the progress of your initiatives are essential. While these can and should be accomplished within your executive suite, it is often useful to get outside opinions as well. External sources are, at the least, unencumbered by direct reporting relationships and empowered to be frank about their assessments.

It is important to choose outside advisors who are credible yet have a different perspective from your internal administrative group. They may, in fact, not be in medical-related fields. Many Phase III leaders develop a cadre of these individuals with whom they work repeatedly such that the external sources develop an understanding of the history and culture of their organizations. Importantly, when used properly, outside confidantes can often give you the most realistic opinion of the way you and your unit are viewed by others. As one experienced leader told us: "When you are engaged in a major initiative, you need to listen to as many outside voices as you can tolerate. You don't need to believe everything they say, as their detailed knowledge of your business may be suboptimal, but you ignore it at your peril."

If you aspire to larger institutional roles, the ability to relate to a wide range of people outside your profession is a key skill. After all, boards of trustees and directors are generally made up of leaders in industries and professions other than medicine or biological sciences. Their insights into management and strategic planning may be different from yours but, more often than not, their input will include options you might not have considered. Further, the process you go through in explaining the situation and your approach is an excellent "dress rehearsal" for when you need to do so to others outside your department.

Redefining Your Relationships with Peers

In a Phase III position, you acquire two new peer groups—your fellow chairs or institute directors at your institution and at others. Your relationship with them will have an important influence on your success.

It may be surprising to learn that you are now far more dependent on the goodwill of your colleagues than when you were leading a more self-contained unit. That said, so much of your value to your department is your ability to navigate the internal politics and facilitate their access to resources. While your department can not expect you to win every decision, you must be able to frame a reasoned argument for their point of view and garner support for meritorious requests. This is best accomplished if you have a mutually supportive relationship with others who might make similar demands.

One experienced departmental chair told us he never turns down a requested favor from one of his fellow chairs as long as it is remotely reasonable. When he is approached, he simply puts himself in the chair's position and commits to solving the problem along with his colleague. "I have found that the returns on this strategy are remarkable. After a few years on the job, not only were my colleagues willing to help me, they developed the habit of routinely banding together to talk through and agree on all key requests before taking them to the dean or hospital president. After banking enough good will, I have gone five years now since I have heard a NO from my fellow chairs. New chairs here pick up the vibe and behave similarly."

Those in parallel positions in other institutions offer a different type of support to the Phase III leader. For one, they can often help benchmark his or her policies and procedures to the norms across the country. As we all tend to face some of the same pressures and challenges, understanding how other institutions are approaching them can inform one's actions.

One of the most difficult interactions is when one practice or institution offers a job to an employee of another. This is slightly more common in academic medicine (the vast majority of academic physicians and scientists change jobs during their career and often more than once) but also occurs commonly in the private practice environment. These career moves have the potential to sour relationships between the employees and the institutions they are leaving and certainly can stress the personal relationships between leaders of the respective practices or departments.

Given the high likelihood of such career decisions, it seems rational to take a less antagonistic view of the process. For one, the desirability of your colleagues or partners is a positive reflection on your mentoring and the environment you have created. Assuming that they are moving up in their new position, changing jobs is the best advertisement that young people can excel in your institution and be strongly considered for other good opportunities. Further, the downside of losing a quality person is mitigated by the opportunity to gain another. If an outstanding young physician or scientist chooses to take another position, a strong institution should be able to restock with someone of equal potential.

An experienced chair had a recent experience with an outstanding mid-level physician who was offered a prestigious section chief position elsewhere. The young man had performed extremely well clinically and in research and clearly had strong leadership skills. When the recruiting institution called for a recommendation on the junior faculty member, the chair was enthusiastic and not defensive. As much as he hated to lose the young man and his many talents, after speaking with him on several occasions during the process, the chair agreed the position was a step up from what could be offered at that time in his department. The move was celebrated as a positive reflection of the caliber of young faculty who were being groomed at the institution and all parties involved remain on friendly terms. Importantly, the newly vacant position was highly sought after and attracted a large number of outstanding applications.

The aforementioned example is perhaps not so unique but does reinforce that the primary vantage point of Phase III leaders should be helping their junior associates determine what is best for them as individuals. Doing so, in word and deed, will reinforce a leader's reputation as a mentor and aide the institution in the long view with subsequent recruitments of other ambitious people.

When is It Time to Move on?

Most organizations value stability and experience in leadership positions. After all, recruitments have actual dollar costs and change disrupts the comfort of many stakeholders. It can also be challenging to maintain enthusiasm for any job after a long period in grade. While a leader can change tactics to respond to new situations, many Phase III leaders acknowledge that there are times when a fundamentally new approach is called for and a different person is required to implement it.

The career patterns of many business leaders are quite different from those in professions such as medicine or law. In business, especially in entrepreneurial settings, leaders move much more frequently, often changing the nature of the enterprise they lead. The premise is that "management is management" irrespective of the field. In some circumstances, owners sell their established businesses and, if financially feasible, take time off before starting a new one.

It is understandable that the years required to acquire the knowledge and experience, which place a Phase III leader at the top of his or her profession, would naturally reduce this kind of mobility in medicine. Still, many of the leaders we spoke with talked about the need to regularly "get outside their comfort zone" to re-energize and renew. A common theme raised was their need to continue to grow in skills and experience. This did not necessarily mean leaving their jobs but frequently did require a change in focus and time allocation motivated by a new role in their institution or in outside professional organizations.

One experienced chair freely admitted that after about 8 years in her job, she noted an increased level of frustration dealing with central administration and worried that she had lost some of the tireless determination necessary to get things accomplished. For several years, she was successful in directing some of her time to service in professional organizations, holding a number of meaningful leadership positions. In these roles, she was able to advocate even more broadly for her priorities in education and physician development. These outside activities were enabled, in part, by the fact that her home department was functioning well. She found that diversifying her attention to national-level problems helped put her local challenges in perspective. Rather than distract her, she clearly felt these outside activities re-invigorated her stewardship of her department. In sum, she again felt like she was accomplishing something in both her personal growth and her contributions to her field.

In other situations, an actual job change is required to restore the joy that accompanies full engagement. Options would include resuming the clinical or research work which provided so much satisfaction earlier in your career, or seeking another administrative role within or outside the institution.

The first path is dependent on your previous success in maintaining your skill set in your core professional areas even as you have devoted more time to administrative work. This means finding a way to avoid becoming only a very occasional clinician or "absentee landlord" in the laboratory. This is not an easy task, given the increased complexity of today's practices and academic departments and the time and effort needed to lead them.

One of the most effective ways of maintaining credibility in clinical or investigative work is to narrow down your interests, while carefully protecting the time that you need to participate in a whole-hearted fashion. In academic endeavors, you will need to continue to make original contributions to the literature, although it is expected that these projects would be collaborative with others, not necessarily requiring you to be the lead. In clinical settings, you might maintain your practice activity by focusing on a specific disease or procedure. In addition to maintaining your credibility, these activities bring you into contact with junior colleagues and give you an excellent opportunity to model the kind of mentoring we like to see in all professional organizations.

One surgical chair told us: "It isn't necessary that I am in the operating room every day, or that I'm regarded as the very best or busiest surgeon in my field; but it is definitely necessary that I can operate well and that the results are good when I do."

As noted earlier, a second option is leaving your job for another administrative position, within your institution or outside. Such a decision must be carefully weighed. Some things to consider are whether the drivers of this move are administrative frustrations that may be short-lived or personal dissatisfactions spilling over and influencing your attitude toward your job. Such situations are common. Indeed, nearly every leader we interviewed admitted to periods of disillusionment with his or her work that lead to considering other options.

Regardless of the situation, one thing is clear. There is little to be gained by sharing your uncertainty with your colleagues. Your peers will invariably interpret this as a lack of full commitment on your part. This may contribute to their loyalty deteriorating (believing you are no longer with them for the long haul). It could also cause them to re-evaluate their own tenure. Unlike the deliberations over strategic and operational challenges, which can often benefit from open discussion, personal reflections over your leadership position should generally remain confidential.

Even worse, you should never use the threat to quit as a bargaining chip unless you are perfectly willing to do so. Such explicit brinksmanship may work on an occasion, but it will eventually erode the confidence others might have in your leadership, especially if it occurs too often (which means more than once a decade!). This is not to say that there *never* are matters of conscience that may be worth putting your job on the line, only that they are not common.

Your colleagues are a final consideration. Most likely many of them relocated to work in your unit or passed on other outside offers to stay there. This surely does not mean that you have an immutable obligation to them forever—they are independent actors and professionals. But, it does require that you seriously consider the effects your actions may have on them.

Chapter 6
Phase IV: Team President

Taking a Phase-IV leadership role represents a fundamental shift in duties. For one, your constituency is almost certain to contain professionals with distinctly different experiences and expertise from your own core competencies. Your initial selection may be based in part on your past achievements, but assessments of your efficacy will be based almost entirely on the success of others and the reputation of your institution. Your job is to further its broader mission by recruiting and retaining talent (human capital) and marshalling the resources they need.

Evaluating the Job

When you are considering an offer to become a dean, president, or CEO, it is important to feel that there is a good cultural fit. This assessment goes well beyond the national reputation of the place or even its stated values and mission. Culture resides in the more subtle elements of day-to-day life, including the manner by which senior leadership and faculty relate to one another. There may be important regional differences, which may be reflected in the social hierarchy and leisure activities. These nuances may not be so easy to decipher during a carefully modulated recruitment process, particularly if you were previously unfamiliar with the institution or health system.

B. L. Gewertz, D. C. Logan, *The Best Medicine,*
DOI 10.1007/978-1-4939-2220-8_6,
© Springer Science+Business Media New York 2015

One of our interviewees described a visit from a Midwestern city to a great university in the Southeast that was recruiting a medical school leader. He was informally contacted by a member of the search committee and invited to meet an influential group of trustees. At 7 a.m. Saturday morning, he journeyed approximately 45 min outside of town to a small gas station. In the back room, six of the most important political and business leaders in the state met weekly over coffee and donuts to build consensus around upcoming university issues. While the candidate was warmly received and was duly impressed with the qualifications and ideas of the group, it was clear that leadership was exercised in a manner quite different from that of his previous experience. He quickly realized that even with well-accepted goals, there would need to be substantial changes in his style and political instincts if he accepted a position here. He was very glad to have had the opportunity to learn this early on in the process.

Insights into the culture can often be inferred by a careful review of the recent history of the leaders who came before you—especially their perceived successes and failures. In fact, the consistency in opinions about the attributes and shortcomings of previous leaders is one good way to determine the degree of alignment of your future colleagues.

Depending on the pace and nature of the recruitment process, you may be exposed to outside stakeholders in the enterprise. These might include community leaders, board members, private unaffiliated physicians, or alumni. To the greatest extent possible, you should use these opportunities to gather candid opinions about the recent performance of the institution and their expectations for it. Strong advocates can become your immediate allies. Less enthusiastic participants may give you important insights into shortcomings not identified in your formal inquiries.

A senior chair was considering a position as senior vice-president and dean of medicine of a state university. He had spent the past 25 years in a private school in a large city with an extremely strong basic research focus. During the recruitment process, both the search committee and the candidate were enthusiastic about the possibilities of increasing the research profile and overall national stature of the school of medicine. Indeed, the candidate's strengths were exactly what the school had not had in a leader.

As negotiations began, the candidate was more broadly exposed to the governing bodies of the school, which included both appointed and elected public officials. His advocacy for a broadening of the student body to insure a wider national representation of academically gifted students (attractive to the academic physicians on the search committee) was viewed as problematic politically, as it would have the potential to decrease the output of home-grown physicians interested in practice within the state. Also, the public trustees were less positive about the investment necessary for expansion of the research enterprise. They were more interested in using available funds to expand the clinical network. The candidate wisely concluded that without external support, especially in the statehouse, it was unlikely his vision could be implemented. The recruitment was terminated. As in many of such situations, both the candidate and the institution have flourished in the past decade, albeit in different arenas.

Negotiating the Job

While it is common for negotiations for Phase III positions to conclude with lengthy and detailed packages of space, money, and other support, Phase IV leaders are expected to generate the resources they need, once given the opportunity. The discussions typically center on having the freedom to do so. In a business analogy, when you are asked to run General Motors, you do not negotiate much. You either want to run a world class automobile company or you do not. Indeed, you will be judged on how well you increase the financial and intellectual capital of the institution. In purely academic settings, the most common mechanisms to increase resources are philanthropy and the recruitment of established scholars with robust research funding. In today's challenging clinical environments, resources are often gained by expanding networks and creating alliances across the care continuum.

"Believe in your ability to create the future."
                                                    -Mark Miller

All About Change

New leaders often come with an expectation of being a change agent. The biggest mistake made by inexperienced Phase IV leaders is a belief that by the force of their personality or through bold administrative maneuvers, they can change an institution profoundly and in short order. Such leaders often learn that schools and health systems have evolved to the way they are because of strong demographic and historical precedents and that even modest changes in policy, emphasis, or function must be carefully managed. Each constituency (alumni, faculty, students, staff) may well have different time courses by which they accommodate to change and these differences must be respected.

An internationally known physician-investigator was recruited to a major research institute. His recruitment was based on the institution's desire to form a medical school. With the strong support of the governing body, he immediately began to seek out the high-level donor needed to make the school financially feasible. Within one year, he gained a large monetary commitment and began to formalize the proposal to obtain temporary accreditation and operational status. A small group of researchers expressed dissatisfaction and lack of support for the venture and a new president was not willing or able to overcome their opposition. The donation disappeared and the idea died. In retrospect, he now realizes that, despite the strong initial board support, he should have involved more of the faculty in the planning, even if that meant the process would have taken considerably more time. When the inevitable conflicts arose, it would have been more difficult to derail the new medical school had its advocacy been more broadly-based.

People's tolerance for change is strongly influenced by the level of personal comfort they have in their leader. There is usually a honeymoon period for the first 6–12 months after senior appointments. Most members of any community want a competent and visionary leader and welcome this possibility. But, until the proper personal connections are solidified, it is wise to move slowly. It is always dangerous when an idea can be characterized as one man's project (and a newcomer's at that!). To properly gauge the open-mindedness of your colleagues, engage in a period of earnest data gathering right from the start. People are far more likely to share their candid views once you have arrived than they might have been during a recruitment process.

> **"People don't care what you know until they know that you care."**
>
> **John Maxwell**

Of course, the difficulty of change certainly does not mean that you should accept the status quo. Indeed, the greatest satisfaction of Phase IV jobs is using your wisdom, judgment, and determination to forge a new path. One could argue that the demands of these jobs are so great that, without such lofty aspiration, they just are not worth doing. Like most athletic pursuits, the trick is letting the game come to you, rather than forcing the action. This does not mean waiting a decade, but a good rule of thumb is to get broad buy-in for your goals before implementing the specific actions to achieve them. This can best be done by focusing on just a few important end points and being persistent in presenting them to the varied audiences you encounter. While you will certainly identify a variance in opinion within the group, you can also count on a base of commonality. After all, the underlying values and mission are what attracted people to teach, practice, and work there. Value-driven individuals generally respond to bold ideas, as long as they are an extension of the historical interests and strengths of an institution. As the influential nineteenth-century architect, city planner, and Director of Works for the 1893 World's Columbian Exposition in Chicago, Daniel Burnham, noted: "Make no little plans. They have no magic to stir men's blood…"

Settling In

One of the most challenging aspects of the transitions to Phase IV jobs is achieving the best balance of strategic and operational work. While you will be properly viewed as responsible and accountable for the full range of problems that can occur across any large organization, it is impossible for you to personally play a major operational role in any consistent manner. Further, you will not have time for such activities, given your other priorities. A substantial amount of your attention must be focused on effectively representing your institution to the *outside*. Your personal work *within* must be focused on a few key initiatives with long-term implications, not the details of operations.

Because of the degree of delegation required and the importance of smooth operations, you will be dependent on the talents and judgments of your administrative colleagues even more than in your previous positions. You must have confidence in them. You may wish to give incumbents some time to demonstrate their capabilities. If and when you determine that their performance is not satisfactory, or even that their personal style is truly incompatible with yours, you must replace them. Such personnel changes must be carried out with sensitivity, as senior administrators invariably have deep and long standing relationships across the institutions they have served. Good faith efforts should be made to secure them different roles within the organization that may be better suited to their skills.

Maintaining a Consistent Public Presence

As chief executive, your attitudes and conduct will be scrutinized by your direct reports as well as by the community at large. As noted in the beginning of our discussion, optimism is a core value of most successful leaders. After all, if you do not expect success, it is awfully hard to convince others of it. This effect is evident in a full range of activities from athletics to musical performances. Visualization of an excellent result is a powerful predictor of achievement. In effect, you must be the one who paints that picture for your entire institution. This does not mean understating the challenges along the way. Rather, you should openly acknowledge them but not make them the focus of your public remarks.

A particularly effective technique is advocated by Harry Davis, professor at the Booth Graduate School of Business of the

University of Chicago. He often begins by asking people, "What would it feel like to be part of the best institution you could imagine?" This is a powerful exercise that focuses on the future and its unlimited possibilities instead of the reasons why such an uplifting state cannot be achieved. Such a conversation tends to bind an audience together, as most people, especially professionals with similar educational backgrounds and responsibilities, share many common views of what would constitute an ideal working environment.

In your advocacy, simpler is always better. Do not send out so many signals that the major and minor points begin to blur; it is far better to maintain a persistent emphasis on the big ideas and allow a wide range of discussion on how to achieve them.

As different parts of your organization may need different strategies and timeframes to accommodate changing expectations, you will be well served to focus early on the intent of your colleagues and to tolerate a range of specific compliance. That said, you should expect their commitment to your joint vision as well as unit-specific strategies to achieve it within certain timeframes.

Be Seen and Be Seen Often

As wonderfully described by college presidents Barry Glassner and Morton Schapiro in a *Wall Street Journal* opinion piece (April 29, 2014), there are few things that are more valued than the physical presence of leaders. "Every constituency wants you to be physically in the room on important occasions; they do not want your surrogate. What you actually do when you get there…may be less important than your physical presence." Your attendance by itself provides participants with unambiguous reinforcement of the value of their efforts. It also links them to the overall mission of the institution, which you embody.

Despite the wisdom of this advice, the need to attend a very large number of events, usually in a ceremonial capacity, can be draining. Your schedule must allow you the time to regroup and refresh. As noted earlier in this book, it is the experience of virtually every busy professional that the opportunities for such renewal simply will not happen if the activities you value are not accorded proper priorities in your schedule.

One unfortunate scenario, which can occur, is the crowding out of social activities other than those which are work related. In a worst case, this can narrow your experience and hurt your perspective.

An experienced physician was appointed hospital CEO of a prominent academic institution during a challenging period. The basic services and amenities of the hospital were thought by some to be lagging behind the overall excellence of the medical care. He set out to change the culture by initiating daily rounds on patient floors to assess and insure the highest level of service. As well, he aggressively pursued fund raising opportunities and various "bridge building" activities in the community. He and his wife soon found that virtually every evening, including weekends, was sub served by his commitments. They made a conscious decision to protect their time with their adolescent children. As an unintended consequence, their other adult social relationships were relegated to a lower priority and essentially disappeared. After a few years, they realized that the lack of "down time" with other adults not related to professional duties was problematic and purposefully rebalanced their scheduling with positive effects.

The aforementioned anecdote is just one example of how the desire to "always be there" can be detrimental. Under the most adverse circumstances, it can lead to the syndrome of professional burn-out, compromising both your job performance and personal development. It is important to remember that irrespective of your administrative capabilities, your most valuable assets are your judgment and accessibility to others. When you are overstressed, these "soft skills" are often the first casualties.

The astronauts who pioneered space flight in the 1960's (described so well in Thomas Wolfe's "The Right Stuff") were under tremendous pressure given the uncertainty of the equipment and the fatal consequences of failure. In response, they relied on the old test pilot concept of "keeping an even strain." In spite of the over controlling supervision of the Mercury space flight administrators, they carved out enough time to do whatever young ambitious risk takers needed to do to maintain some type of balance.

There are few of us with major professional responsibilities who have not found ourselves overcommitted on occasion. The trick is having the internal warning system to recognize the situation and address it. It is even better if you can process these experiences in a more generalized manner and learn to actively balance your time and efforts to avoid such situations.

What About Professional Credibility

At these highest levels of leadership, finding time to continue your clinical or scholarly work is problematic and, at times, even risky. The amount of time and attention required to do the quality of work which established your professional reputation just is not there.

In our interviews, we heard a number of leaders express their regret that such a blending of activities was not easier. They also noted that the risks of performing in a less than stellar fashion were substantial. Poor or even mediocre academic or clinical performances could undermine your reputation in your leadership role. Physician leaders often found it difficult to stay up to date on relevant clinical or research advances. Those previously enjoying active clinical practices often found that their skills surely did not improve with less frequent exposure to patients. Research-based leaders commented that the challenges of their administrative roles intruded on the "thinking time" required for creative scholarship.

Some limited involvement is possible. One university president selected a narrow area of expertise and regularly made the time to teach part of a course on the subject. Another CEO attended laboratory meetings as frequently as possible. A hospital president maintained a small clinical practice, acting solely as a diagnostician rather than the surgeon he was during the bulk of his career. While the principle benefit of continuing your academic activities is intellectual stimulation, more than one leader commented on the credibility they gained by their engagement in the primary functions of the enterprise.

The over-riding lesson of these experiences is that continued involvement in your academic field is desirable if realistically calibrated. Even if limited in scope, such activities visibly align you with institutional missions. Further, you can get insights into the real life of your colleagues, students, or patients which cannot be accessed from your executive suite.

Gender Issues

In the previous chapters, we did not directly address the different experiences of leaders related to gender. Doubtless, gender has many subtle and not so subtle influences on both style and strategy. Indeed, a text equal in length to this one would be only a start in addressing in the subject.

It is not surprising that, in our research, gender issues were rarely raised by male leaders. The female leaders we interviewed also tended to downplay the challenges, perhaps a reflection of the indomitable spirit which accounted for their advancement. Still, a number of them commented that in many settings, especially when convened with others in similar leadership positions, they felt the disquiet of being outnumbered. They did note that clear efforts were being made by professional development courses to include issues specific to female leaders. Female leaders frequently voiced their responsibility to advocate for more equal advancement of women in their fields and better access to leadership roles. As well expressed by one experienced medical leader: "We are all about giving people a chance. A chance to survive, a chance to serve, a chance to excel. We should not tolerate it when half of our population does not get that opportunity."

In Phase IV leadership positions, another aspect of gender comes into play. As pointed out by Karen Lawrence, President of Sarah Lawrence, the spouse of a Phase IV leader is invariably expected to play an important role in social activities both within the institution and in the community at large. As indicated by many of our interviewees, the more prominent your leadership position, the more involvement is required. The significance of this spousal support is much better appreciated by female leaders than their male counterparts. Further, the availability of a male spouse is apt to be more problematic due to a higher incidence of concurrent job responsibilities.

Chapter 7
Phase V: Sports Commissioner/ League Founders

Phase V is all about reinvention and occurs when an extraordinary leader at Phase IV decides to change the nature of the field from which he or she emerged. Very few leaders ever get to Phase V. Those who do become household names: Steve Jobs (technology), Richard Branson (travel), Warren Buffet (value investing), and Elon Musk (travel and innovation-based investing). In each case, transformational leaders end up affecting the lives of millions of people.

The difficulty in writing this chapter is that, so far, medicine has produced very few "league founders." Even in fields that produced many more (e.g., technology or finance), the road each has taken is unique. However, by examining the history of transformational innovation and leadership, it is possible to tease out the skills, mindset, and behaviors that led the person to find his or her own path.

Reflection, Reason, and Rhetoric

Dave has spent much of his life studying transformational leaders in all fields. One of the biggest insights from this study is that leaders who change the core functioning of a field—who are "disruptors"—are almost universally good at three core skills: reflection about their own lives and choices others have made, reasoning through trends and opportunities, and sharing the result of both through persuasive communication. Our shorthand for these three skills is reflection, reason, and rhetoric.

B. L. Gewertz, D. C. Logan, *The Best Medicine*, 73
DOI 10.1007/978-1-4939-2220-8_7,
© Springer Science+Business Media New York 2015

These three skills are parallel rather than serial, meaning the transformational leader is doing all three all the time. Initial conversations (rhetoric) with people become ways to test the soundness of reason and authenticity that comes from deep reflection. Reason is a way to connect the feedback of others with the person's core convictions discovered through reflection. Reflection keeps people from being too cerebral (too much reason) or too ego-driven when rhetoric connects them to mass audiences.

The insight that these three skills are required in the same person has important implications for physicians aspiring to lead their field through disruption of the status quo. Most professionals begin their careers by emphasizing individual or team performance, or reaching mass audiences, but not both. Further, people who make one career choice often look down on people who have made the other choice. Bestselling authors (good at rhetoric) look at academics as being narrow and overly analytical, while academics (good at reason) look at people with a large base of readers or viewers or social media followers as being sell-outs. The key is to use reflection as the mediator between reason and rhetoric because only periods of quiet can bring a person back to their *True North*, as Bill George wrote in the book of that title.

While the three skills—reflection, reason, and rhetoric—are all done at once, we were struck by how a period of reflection often led people to take stock of their lives, and how this quiet period seemed to prepare them for what was to follow. Steve Jobs was famously fired by the computer company he founded and, in the resulting period of introspection, he found a new passion for media. This focus served him well when he returned to Apple and helped their transition from a computer maker to one of the most famous brands in history.

A good example of a phase V medical leader is Eric Topol. Eric was a highly distinguished academic cardiologist, who progressed rapidly from leading the cardiac catheterization laboratory at the University of Michigan (in his 30's) to serving as the founding Dean of a new medical school at the Cleveland Clinic. After moving to Scripps Institute in San Diego to be Director of the Translational Science Institute in 2006, Eric became even more focused on the power of genomics in the diagnosis and treatment of heart disease and other common illnesses. He had long studied the subject—beginning as early as his undergraduate days—and had founded one of the first cardiovascular gene banks in 1996. He also saw the expanded capabilities of wireless technology and became the most visible and articulate advocate for using the power of handheld computing in medicine. He showed how patients could easily monitor their own heart rhythms and cardiac function and communicate effortlessly with physicians and other caregivers. His best-selling book, The Creative Destruction of Medicine, made a persuasive case for the value of wireless monitoring and genomic studies in lowering the cost of care while enhancing patient and doctor satisfaction. Eric's well-selected media appearances and obvious passion for the subjects have inspired many young physicians, engineers, and programmers to advance the field. In doing so, he has extended his influence far beyond his institution and even exceeded the considerable impact of his scientific work.

Making the Simple Complex, and the Complex Simple

All radical change starts with a new way of seeing an old problem—in short, an insight. In our study of transformational leaders, most have the ability to take a situation that everyone seems to understand, and find new ways of explaining what happened and why. Likewise, when others are lost in the detail of a situation, the same leaders come up with a brilliantly simple solution. In both cases, leaders are contrarians—complicating what appears to be simple, and simplifying what seems to be complex.

Elon Musk of SpaceX and Tesla Motors is a great example. Rather than bemoan the demise of the American space program, he sought a solution that would provide cheaper and more reliable space travel. After several failed attempts, which almost bankrupted SpaceX, he had a successful launch and, soon after, a lucrative contract with National Aeronautics and Space Administration.

More recently, Musk sought to make electric cars elegant, resulting in Tesla Motors. Not satisfied with his innovation to date, he is now considering a simple question: why has airline travel changed so little since the 1960's? The reason, he decided, is the problematic nature of supersonic travel—it is loud, potentially destructive (by creating a sonic boom) and expensive (in jet fuel). He, thus, reasoned that a near vacuum tube (a simple solution) would eliminate all these problems at once. Musk has expressed interest in a $6 billion tube connecting Los Angeles and San Francisco, and a more ambitious program to connect the east and west coasts of the United States. In both cases, travel would be faster, cleaner, and much more energy efficient than with commercial airlines.

Finding Freedom on the Other Side of Constraint

Phases I through IV are all about learning a new set of rules and letting go of the rules of the previous phase. The same is true with Phase V with one big difference: the rules at this last phase are self-imposed. The difficulty for anyone at this level is unlearning the constraints that made someone successful at the prior phases.

Studies on creativity lead to a fascinating conclusion: to be effective, creativity needs to come after learning, and then letting go, of constraints on original thinking. Consider young children. They want to create—on the walls, with their food (often on the walls), and in what they wear (or do not wear). Yet, they do not know enough for this creativity to be useful. Years of education follow, in which they are taught the structure of language, math, science, and other subjects. Later, they pick a subject to specialize in and, in most fields, are only encouraged to really create at the end of a doctorate degree when they have mastered the important work of those who came before them. They may decide to go into industry, when they learn more constraints about how organizations work and how to behave in management and executive meetings. Only when they get to the top of a company are they encouraged to lead and to change the status quo. The problem is every step of learning builds a trained incapacity to create something new. So, when a person reaches the ideal spot from which to innovate—after education and years of following others in an organization—their ability to create is at a career low.

A child experiments with clothes, mismatching polka dots and plaids, yet, a designer who may mix these same patterns is doing so to create a conscious work of art. The designer's creativity is informed by the rules she is breaking.

Likewise, the challenge of finding the freedom of Phase V is in "unlearning" constraint—and only then do the years of preparation become a base for something truly original. The pattern of this book is: learn the rules, follow the rules, and then rewrite the rules. Phase V is for the rewriters.

Begin with No End in Mind

There is no Phase VI, but there are different levels of impact within V. If we look at Phase V across industries, most leaders who get to this level create transformational change once—and then falter. It is for this reason that Steve Jobs, Richard Branson, and Elon Musk are so notable—each has produced lightning strikes multiple times.

For leaders in Phase V, the only choices are to settle into routine or continue self-reinvention. Plateauing early is often a result of the *Innovator's Dilemma* (Clayton Christensen's concept from a book with that title): when "doing the right thing is the wrong thing." As start-ups become established, they naturally become more conservative and risk-averse and roles become more established and rigid. Choosing the conventional moves makes a less nimble organization, leaving the company vulnerable to attacks from without.

The Phase V leader should be especially alert to the problem of control. Predictably, such innovators attract other revolutionaries, who do not like to be put in a box. So, as the Phase V leader grows an organization, the question is: should that new group be allowed to slow down innovation or should it disrupt itself? And for the leader at the helm, should that person disrupt what made him or successful?

The Inevitability of Disruption

Late in December, 2010, Peter H. Diamandis, a medical doctor and Chairman and CEO of the XPRIZE Foundation met with Qualcomm's Don Jones to discuss whether technology was at a point where a Star Trek "tricorder" was possible. A few months later, the $10 million Qualcomm Tricorder XPRIZE was announced, in which the first team to produce such a device would receive $10 million.

The language announcing the prize was telling: "In virtually every industry, end consumer needs drive advances and improvements, except in healthcare. Very few methods exist for consumers to receive direct medical care without seeing a healthcare professional at a clinic or hospital, creating an access bottleneck. Despite substantial investment to improve the status quo, even average levels of service, efficiency, affordability, accessibility, and satisfaction remain out of reach for many whom the system was intended to help. A prize is thus sorely needed."

Medicine, in our opinion, will be disrupted, in much the same way that change has upended music, newspapers, books, movies, and education. So far, technological shifts in healthcare have mostly resulted in augmentations to the basic model that defines the roles of physicians, hospitals, medical groups, pharmacies, insurance companies, and payers. We believe, more radical change is about to hit healthcare.

> **"Lead, follow or get out of the way."**
> **Thomas Paine**

The question is: who will do the disrupting? Our hope is that it will be physicians and specifically those doctors that have climbed the professional ladder outlined in this book.

While most disruption starts with experts in technology, it is important to see that radical change in other professions has come from the inside. Many of the thinkers who are disrupting computers and software are themselves engineers. Macro changes in the legal profession have been pioneered by attorneys, with two in five United States senators being members of the bar. Warfare looks nothing like it did 200 years ago, but the changes in the military have been led by military officers.

It is interesting to note that while Peter Diamandis has an MD from Harvard, he never completed a residency. He told Dave that he uses the thinking he got in medical school every day, but decided that the better way to change the world was to forge his own road.

Our concern is that medicine is a unique profession, grounded in core values and with a sacred commitment to patients. Famously, Steve Jobs met with recording artists, as teams at Apple worked on the iPod and iTunes. Jobs said many times that he was able to lead a revolution in music because he and others at Apple loved music. The same principle applied when Apple began to disrupt television and movies; after all, Jobs had run Pixar. Microsoft, he said, was filled with technologists who did not love what they were attempting to disrupt, and never found market traction for their solutions.

We hope that those leaders who oversee the transition in healthcare will be those who love the profession of medicine, and have led it as a team player, team captain, and team president.

Chapter 8
A Leader's Guide to the Phases

This book is a vertical examination of physician leadership. Each phase is its own world, with a "coin of the realm" (what is valued at that level), rules, customs, and signs that a leader is ready for the next phase.

The big message of this book is to get to know yourself, learn the phases, and find the best fit. Move toward that ideal phase by completing all the work in the earlier phases, one at a time. Even if a certain phase seems ideal for you, leave open the possibility that you will go further. Many of the people we interviewed at Phase III and higher said that they had never guessed they would run something so large and intricate.

There are other lessons for all physician leaders, regardless of where they are in their career or how high they intended to go. This chapter goes through that advice.

Go from *What* to *How* to *Wow*!

As a long-time student of leadership development, Dave has noticed a general trend in professions: highly educated people tend to move from "what" to "how" to "wow!"

B. L. Gewertz, D. C. Logan, *The Best Medicine,*
DOI 10.1007/978-1-4939-2220-8_8,
© Springer Science+Business Media New York 2015

People in the first half of their career are rewarded primarily for "what"—accomplishments and results. How they get those results matters, but less so. Phase I in this book is about "what." For people who will move into later phases of leadership, the "how" they get things done is important, but less than the results themselves.

Roughly half-way through their career, the rules change, but no one tells them. The change is obvious much later, but not at the time. The shift is that "what" and "how" invert in importance. Results still matter, but "how" those results are achieved matters as much, and often, much more. Phases II through IV are about the "how," with "how" increasing in importance in the later phases.

A few individuals go further, into the "wow!" part of their career. They emphasize and attempt to leverage the trends that will reshape an industry. This insight hit Dave nearly 15 years into the USC Master of Medical Management. In each class, there was almost always one person who could amaze (and scare) the others by pointing out how things were about to change. Approximately 12 years ago, a student commented how U.S.-trained radiologists in India might begin to read scans overnight for a much lower cost. Later, these "wow!" individuals pointed to trends in telemedicine, or to the unsustainability of healthcare as it neared 20% of gross domestic product. Nearly 10 years ago, one person asked a class: "How many of you would encourage your kid to become a physician?" Almost no hands went up. He then described what medicine would probably look like 20 years from that point, in terms of bundled payments, with fee-for-service becoming a thing of the past. Today he is running a technology company that is promoting wellness through smartphone apps.

In recent years, that one person in every class began to speak of changes in medicine that parallel what happened to the music industry, or to newspapers, years ago. Dave learned about the Qualcomm "Tricorder" XPRIZE from one of those MMM students, and first heard a refrain that is now common (and controversial): in 10 years, an iPhone with $20 of additional peripheries might replace a primary care visit.

The takeaway here is: know where you are in your career. Plan for the next phase. Adopt its rules before it becomes glaringly obvious that you have waited too late. If you want to move to a later phase, demonstrate the skills and behaviors of it as evidence that you will do that job well.

Tribes Up, Down, and Sideways

In each phase, you must build peer relationships with those in the same phase as you. It is critical to learn what the "coin of the realm" is, as it will have changed from the prior phase. Phase I is about expertise and narrow results. Phase II is about departmental excellence and also the ability to hit revenue/expense targets. Phase III concerns itself with national reputations in which your group must compete against the best national and international players. In Phase IV, the "coin of the realm" becomes leading the field of medicine. Phase V is about reinventing healthcare.

A simple technique for emphasizing that you are a member of a team (or tribe), rather than a solo performer, is to shift your pronoun from "I" to "we." What "we" refers to specifically will change throughout your career, as you move from team player to team captain to coach to team president to league founder.

At each phase, you will need to manage and lead groups one, two, three, or even four phases behind you. The key to your behavior is to hold people accountable for the rules which apply to their phase, not the one you occupy.

A major challenge in managing down is that your opinion of others will go a long way to determining their potential for advancement ("promotability"). Some early readers have asked what to do if a person wants to move to the next phase but is not ready and may never be ready. Here, we have to recall advice Jack Welch gave when he ran GE—that the most inhumane action of all is to send the message (implicitly or explicitly) that someone can be promoted, when such a move is not in the cards. Giving such pointed advice must be thought through, however. It is possible that you need the person in that role. It is also possible that your opinion of their abilities may change. Or that when it is time to consider a move up, that you will not be the decision maker any longer. For these reasons, it is important to send a message which reflects only the moment in which you deliver it. Your opinion may change, or it may not be the critical opinion.

At the same time, you will need to be a part of teams that are led by someone in the phase above yours. To serve in that position as effectively as possible, learn the "coin of the realm" of the next phase. Doing so prepares you for possible promotion, as it distinguishes you from peers who will likely stay where they are. Also, the more you think above your phase, the more you can lead and serve those who report to you.

Defer the Decision on How Far to Go in Your Own Career

Some people who read this book prior to publication attempted to answer the question: "How far should I go?" for themselves. It is a great question to try answer early in one's career. And an even better question to leave open.

Our best advice is to stay open to the possibility of the next phase, even if you seem to be a perfect fit where you are. The best way to "kick the tires" on the next phase is by developing professional relationships with those in the next phase. Learn what is important from their perspective. See the problems and opportunities.

We suggest finding ways to network that bring you into contact with physicians at later phases. Ideal positions are board positions in associations, especially leadership roles in local or state medical associations. Many of Dave's MMM students have gone for board positions in the American College of Physician Executives and have thus met physician leaders from across the country.

You want exposure to people at the next phase when you and they are working on a common problem, rather than in networking sessions that can be awkward. For that reason, find where physicians in the next phase spend their time. They may be nonprofit leaders in causes that are not directly related to their jobs, such as on a local Red Cross board or on the Boys & Girls club.

Our biggest admonition, however, is to always be professional, and err on the side of caution. Nothing is more acidic to career prospects than coming across as a weird stalker.

Make Promotion of Stars a Top Priority

In the USC Master of Medical Management, Dave makes it a point to spot the individuals who have the interests, values, and capacity to go further. Many appear to be waiting for someone to give them permission to shoot higher. He has found an ideal way for these conversations to begin is to go to dinner with several other students. Go around the table and have them all discuss where they are in their career and why they entered the USC program. When a person who should go to the next phase says that he or she is just in the program for his own development, the other students usually say the person should consider aiming for another job. In many cases, these conversations lead to the person going for another job, with the strong recommendation of a fellow classmate.

The point of the story is that human beings are social creatures, who need external feedback to tell us where we fit the best. So, one way to read this book is to help you find your ideal career fit and aim for that phase. A better way to read it is to consider all the people around you—at the same phase, and above, and below—and ask where they fit. Physicians who develop a reputation for developing others find it much easier to move to where they want to go.

Do Not Take Shortcuts

In Dave's and Bruce's 50 plus combined years as educators and leaders, they have seen many talented individuals plateau earlier in their career than their values and abilities would have predicted. The most common reason is attempting to cut corners, including seeking promotion before a person has learned the important lessons in a phase. Some of Dave's MMM students return to school to attempt to make up for a weakness from such an early promotion.

This problem is especially acute in academic medicine. Do not leave Phase I until you have distinguished yourself as a researcher or master clinician. If you do, your lack of prowess will hurt you until you get to Phase IV. Do not leave Phase II until you have made the group you lead far superior to what it was when you took over or you will be seen as "failing your way to the top." Do not leave Phase III until the place you led is distinguished in some key way that was not seen as likely when you took over. Do not leave Phase IV until you can point to at least one major accomplishment as proof you can lead.

Do Not Linger Too Long

The aforementioned advice must be balanced against the opposite concern: appearing to loiter too long in a position. There is a point in each phase when you "own" it. Continued success is easy—and boring. Almost always, this moment comes after years of hardship, of winning people over to a new strategy, and of key hires. At this point, it is important to stake stock of your position from a perspective of what will serve others the most. We suggest three questions to guide you about whether to stay or move on.

First, what would happen if you left—suddenly, right now? Someone will move into your role, or into new roles defined as a result of your departure. These will be new opportunities for people, chances for them to grow and become stronger leaders. Assess whether you have the right people in place to take over. And if you do, consider that it might best serve everyone for you to leave. Sometimes, the best leadership play one can make is to disappear.

Second, is it possible to advance to the next phase in the role you are currently in? Warren Bennis once told Dave that you can see that a revolution has taken place not because the roles change, but because the relationship between the roles is different. He noted that after the Magna Carta, the UK still had a king (or queen), but the relationship between the monarch and parliament was forever shifted. Today, a revolution in healthcare is underway. Private practices are being bought and sold, with new relationship networks forming and old alliances being undone. The role of hospitals and insurance companies is changing and the relationship between these roles is changing faster.

Many physicians find themselves having more career options than ever before. As you sort through the shifting career possibilities, consider whether you can stay in your current job *and* advance to the next phase at the same time. Many private practice physicians are entering hospitals and finding themselves in powerful committee roles. Many academic medicine physicians are entering administration, balancing research and teaching roles with Phase II, III, or even IV leadership positions.

There are numerous examples of how physicians have utilized their creativity to illuminate important health care issues to a wider audience. Jerome Groopman and Atul Gawande from Harvard University are just two recent examples of physicians who have maintained active practices (in oncology and endocrine surgery) while writing for acclaimed periodicals. Their message of appropriate care and safety has reached a broad audience within the profession and outside. In this fashion, they have also greatly expanded their personal influence on society.

In times of rapid change, look to where things are going rather than historical precedents. Today's rapid shifts in role relationships would have been unimaginable 10 years ago. Likewise, the relational web 10 years from now would be unrecognizable today. As the probably apocryphal Wayne Gretzky quote goes: "Skate to where the puck is going to be, not where it has been."

Build Your Career on a Set of Core Values that Will not Change

Dave's study of organizations reveals that people misunderstand what changes and what needs to remain the same. Apple Computer, when it was founded in a garage, stood for innovation and cool technology—as it sold Apple II computers that loaded programs from a cassette tape player. Apple, after it dropped "Computer" from its name, stands for innovation and cool technology—by selling iPhones and media through its online store. The story is that technology changes, but the most important elements do not change. In a famous address to Apple employees, Steve Jobs introduced the "Think Different" advertising campaign that foreshadowed the company's move into consumer electronics. Ironically, he said the company's message is about what should not change, not about what was shifting. In his words: "The question [in the advertisement] we asked was, our customers want to know what we stand for. They want to know where we fit in this world. And, what we're about isn't making boxes to get their jobs done, although we do that well...Apple is about something more than that. Apple at the core, its core value, is that we believe that people with passion can change the world for the better."

Harvard's Clayton Christensen has spent his life studying industry change as described in his landmark book *The Innovator's Dilemma*. Later books focused on disruption in industries he considers to be the most important to human life: education (*Disrupting Class*) and healthcare (*The Innovator's Prescription*). Throughout his study, he keeps returning to what should not change. In his words: "Decide what you stand for. And then stand for it all the time." Christensen devoted a book to this concept: *How Will You Measure Your Life?*

As you consider what is changing in healthcare, we recommend you go back to *your* core, to *your* core value. Why did you decide to become a physician? What first interested you in leadership? A core value is a basis on which to make a decision. The same core value should guide you as you navigate the changing realities of the industry. The key to change is keeping core values constant even when everything else shifts around.

Your Final Step in a Phase is Making Yourself Replaceable

Each phase has a beginning, middle, and end. Most of this book focuses on the beginning (establishing yourself) and the middle (making the role your own). The end is about succession planning: finding and grooming one or more people to replace you.

This chapter focuses on common mistakes people make in the phases, such as taking shortcuts or premature promotions. There is one more error to consider: making your organization dependent on you in your current role.

Dave spends a large part of his time in small roundtable meetings of healthcare C suite executives. One of the most common problems they raise is their own succession—because the people who are most able to run an organization are needed in some lower position—dean, director, vice provost, etc. The conversation is ironic, of course, because the advice for the person in the roundtable is the same as for the person they are considering for a higher role. Every leader's job includes succession planning, and one person who has not found and trained a replacement creates a problem all the way up through the hierarchy.

Your role is therefore twofold. First, make yourself replaceable. Second, make every person below you replaceable. If you fail in either part of this task, you risk holding yourself and others back.

We consider succession planning as the last step in each phase, a sort of final exam before graduation to the next role. The question is: can you develop someone else to be more effective in your role, than you are?

Always Pay Attention to the Phase V Leaders

With all the changes in healthcare, everyone's attention needs to look to those who are redrawing the relationships between the roles. As we wrote in the last chapter, we hope that change in healthcare will be driven by leaders from within the profession of medicine. But regardless of who does the redrawing, pay attention to those "disruptors" who are changing everything.

Change starts by finding a new and cheaper way to solve a problem that can quickly scale across a population. Disruptors in healthcare can come from anywhere: technology, government, business, or medicine. We strongly advise physician leaders to watch for those trends that will begin small and then explode out. Here, we can only rely on analogies. Taxi drivers needed to look out for Uber. Newspaper editors needed to watch for Huffington

Post for "free" journalism and Craigslist for competition for classified ads. College administrators need to watch out for TED. In each case, the idea behind the change was "democratization"—making something available for low or no cost that used to be only be accessible to small groups. Before Uber, only the wealthy could text a driver to pick them up. Before Huffington Post, people had to pay for a newspaper to read leading op-ed writers. Before TED, only handfuls of people could hear thought-leaders in small classes at elite universities.

Change in healthcare will follow similar roads. Look for moves to democratize and scale healthcare. Remember that changes begin with products and services that are "not ready for primetime." Then, each release gets incrementally better. The new versions come out faster and faster. Before most people realize anything has changed, everything is different.

Our final comment to physicians is to remember the sacredness of the physician–patient relationship. Shifting economics, advancing technologies, and changes in regulation will redefine the role of the physician. But, the purity of that relationship will never change...unless physician leaders allow it to change.

We hope you will become one of those leaders who brings about healthy change, while remaining true to the ancient commitments of the founders of this profession.

Index

B. L. Gewertz, D. C. Logan, *The Best Medicine,*
DOI 10.1007/978-1-4939-2220-8,
© Springer Science+Business Media New York 2015